Jazz and Cocktails

Jazz and Cocktails

RETHINKING RACE AND THE
SOUND OF FILM NOIR

Jans B. Wager

University of Texas Press   *Austin*

Requests for permission to reproduce material from this work should be
sent to:

Permissions
University of Texas Press
P.O. Box 7819
Austin, TX 78713-7819
http://utpress.utexas.edu/index.php/rp-form

♾ The paper used in this book meets the minimum requirements of
ANSI/NISO Z39.48-1992 (R1997) (Permanence of Paper).

LIBRARY OF CONGRESS CATALOGING-IN-PUBLICATION DATA

Names: Wager, Jans B., 1958– author.
Title: Jazz and cocktails : rethinking race and the sound of film noir /
Jans B. Wager.
Description: First edition. | Austin : University of Texas Press, 2017. |
Includes bibliographical references and index.
Identifiers: LCCN 2016022320
    ISBN 978-1-4773-1226-1 (cloth : alk. paper)
    ISBN 978-1-4773-1227-8 (pbk. : alk. paper)
    ISBN 978-1-4773-1228-5 (library e-book)
    ISBN 978-1-4773-1229-2 (non-library e-book)
Subjects: LCSH: Jazz in motion pictures. | Film noir—History and
criticism. | Race in motion pictures. | Sound in motion pictures. |
Motion pictures and music.
Classification: LCC PN1995.9.J37 W34 2017
DDC 791.43/6578—dc23
LC record available at https://lccn.loc.gov/2016022320

doi:10.7560/312261

For my sisters, Tracy and Deidra

Contents

Acknowledgments

MANY PEOPLE HELPED AND SUPPORTED ME THROUGH-
out the process of researching and writing this book. I
wish to thank the student researchers and assistants, including Rikki
Carter, Jana Arbuckle, Van Zetrus, Tim Dawson, and Zoe McDonald,
and I am grateful to friends and colleagues who read chapters or assisted
with the project, including Drs. Nathan Gorelick, Rick McDonald, Grant
Moss, Ryan Simmons, Brian Whaley, Anne Pelzel, Maria Pramaggiore,
Krin Gabbard, Bill Luhr, Eric Pierson, as well as Katherine McIntyre,
and Laurie Wood. Thanks to my friend, Kismet Rasmussen, to Maria Pramaggiore for her brilliance and encouragement, and Krin Gabbard for
his friendship and insight. I'm very grateful to Dr. Rob Carney for his
assistance and to Drs. Steve Gibson and David Yells, as well as others at
Utah Valley University (UVU), who supported my continued scholarship.
UVU also provided scholarships, fellowships, and sabbaticals throughout
the project. Thanks to Lee Witten at the Ogden Union Station Archive, to
Greg Walsh and Barbara Hall at the Margaret Herrick Library, to Mark
Quigley at the UCLA Film and Television Archive, and to Mary Naylor at
the UVU Library. Thanks also to Jim Burr, at University of Texas Press, for
his ongoing help and backing. Thanks to Betty Moore and Joe McQueen
who graciously spent time answering my questions. Thanks to my family,
and especially my sisters, Deidra and Tracy, who always support my endeavors. Particular thanks to Tracy for her graphic skills on the images and
for moving to Utah. I am grateful to Dimitrije Milovich for his encouragement and so much more.

Permissions

Permissions were kindly granted by the following organizations and individuals:

Alfred Music Publishing and Reservoir Media Music for the use of lyrics from "Lush Life"

Van Summerill for use of the 1947 photograph of Peery's Egyptian Theater in Ogden

Literature/Film Quarterly for permission to use material from my essay "Jazz and Cocktails: Reassessing the Black and White Mix in Film Noir," previously published in *Literature/Film Quarterly* 35:2 (2007)

Joe L. McQueen for inclusion in the project

Betty Stuart Moore for inclusion in the project

Lee Witten and the Ogden Union Station Archive for the use of historical photographs

Jazz and Cocktails

Introduction

NOSTALGIA FOR THE LUSH LIFE

*T*HE TITLE OF THIS VOLUME PAYS HOMAGE TO "LUSH Life," the melancholy jazz song by William "Billy" Strayhorn, written when he was in his late teens or early twenties. Strayhorn, a jazz composer, arranger, and pianist, a social activist, and a gay man, worked closely with Edward Kennedy "Duke" Ellington, including collaborating with Ellington on *Anatomy of a Murder* (1959), which I discuss in chapter 7. The song opens with the lines, "I used to visit all the very gay places, / Those come what may places / Where one relaxes on the axis / Of the wheel of life / To get the feel of life / From jazz and cocktails."[1] Some read the lines, "I used to visit all the very gay places, / Those come what may places," as indicative of Strayhorn's homosexual lifestyle, but David Hajdu, in his biography of Strayhorn, notes that the young musician "would not have been likely to use the word gay to signify same-sex romance in 1933."[2] My favorite version of the song, and likely the most famous, is on the album *Lush Life*, which features Johnny Hartman's smooth singing and John Coltrane's saxophone. For me, the song evokes the nostalgic mood, smoky clubs, and endless doomed love affairs of many noir films. In fact, my interest in jazz came after my obsession with film noir.

The tough guys and equally tough, beautiful female protagonists, the hard-boiled dialog and plots, the black-and-white cinematography, the feeling of postwar ennui that infused films noirs—all this presented a seductive visual and narrative alternative to the rest of the Hollywood fare from the 1940s and 1950s, and it continues to fascinate film lovers today. Listening attentively to the music in these films never occurred to me, except when the music insisted, as in Rita Hayworth's performance of "Put the Blame on Mame" in *Gilda* (1946). I started to hear film music only when I turned my scholarly attention to jazz, which resonated with me as an adult listener. I started with Miles Davis, John Coltrane, Charles Mingus, then Ben Webster and Dexter Gordon on my turntable, and as I became more interested, I began to expand my repertoire. As an aficionada, not a scholar or musician, I read about the musicians, about their relentless artistry, and about how racism shaped their lives. Only then did I begin thinking about jazz in film noir. As Kathryn Kalinak notes, my lack of real awareness of film music ties precisely into "the transcendent power of the image and the dependence of the soundtrack."[3] Because music functions primarily as amplification for the narrative, it is easy not to notice the auditory as much as the visual. And film noir's visual attractions, with its gorgeous and dangerous femmes and hommes fatals, abound.

Classic film noir resists Hollywood's drive for heterosexual romantic unions. Although good had to triumph over evil, thanks to the industry's censorship board, the Production Code Administration (PCA), the triumph was fraught with ambiguity. Spectator sympathy often resided with the alluring, embattled, and criminal characters rather than the law-abiding ones. Nevertheless, the music in classic film noir hewed closely to classical Hollywood scoring practices. Like Kalinak, Claudia Gorbman suggests that in most Hollywood films, music "is subordinated to the narrative's demands," and relegated to supporting the emotive content.[4] *Jazz and Cocktails* will suggest that, especially in late classic films noirs, the musical discourse of jazz intensifies and magnifies intellectual values, sometimes in conflict with the emotional values embedded in the cinematic narrative. Jennifer Fleeger, discussing jazz and opera in early Hollywood sound film, contradicts the notion, common to theorists such as Kalinak and Gorbman, of the subordination of sound to image in classical Hollywood. For Fleeger, the early film spectator already knew jazz and opera as popular music, and this background awareness helped the viewer accept the innovative presence of sound in the cinema. Fleeger goes on to suggest that "opera and jazz are not mere kernels of recognition but . . . shape the score and can derail the authority of the gaze."[5]

So a spectator might hear film music actively as a separate discourse from, or as an adjunct to, the visual narrative. This depends on the viewer's experience of the movie and prior experience of the music. As I note, at first I saw more than I heard film noir. But in late classic film noir, the soundtracks implicate the social and cultural context of jazz music and composers, adding a revolutionary, if short-lived, element to late classical Hollywood filmmaking practice. I am arguing for a theorized spectator who might be active, knowledgeable about jazz, and capable of reading a film's music separately from the narrative, but I am aware that paradigm does not describe all spectators. I explore jazz as a discourse that works both ways, as suturing element, implicating the spectator in the narrative, and as an element that separates itself from film narrative. I start and end with Duke Ellington and Billy Strayhorn, and travel through Utah, Mexico, Paris, New York, and Los Angeles, "all the very gay places."[6]

Using actual jazz clubs or their representations in film as an organizing principle for my exploration, I begin with Pie Eye's Juke Joint: Jazz and Its Interpretations. Pie Eye is the name of Ellington's character in *Anatomy of a Murder*.[7] I explore the meaning of jazz in early classic film noir and suggest how that meaning changed from the early 1940s to the late 1950s. I introduce two possible ways to hear and see jazz in late classic noir, Afromodernism and the alienation effect. Afromodernism allows a reading that focuses on black activism and the use of innovation and integration to achieve artistic goals in white Hollywood. The alienation effect suggests a more general understanding of the type of disruption within established codes that jazz offered to Hollywood soundtracks. In chapter 2, "The Porters and Waiters Club: Jazz, Movies, and Ogden," I use Utah to establish a non-Hollywood context for my study. I explore how the state in which I currently live and work—just west of middle America and located on the east–west train lines during the noir years—served as a stopping-off point for many jazz greats as they traversed the country. Utah also served as home to African Americans, including jazzman Joe McQueen, cousin of saxophonist Herschel Evans, and Betty Moore, cousin of trumpeter Art Farmer. I consider what made Ogden, Utah, a viable residence for Joe and Betty. Joe played with Charlie Parker, helped to integrate the clubs in Utah and Wyoming, and still plays a few times a month at a local Ogden club as well as Salt Lake City clubs. Joe's skill as a saxophone player supplemented his other employment as a mechanic and porter at the central train station. Betty—whose husband, a former Harlem Globetrotter, was, until 2013, a barber on Twenty-Fifth Street in Ogden—was an avid moviegoer throughout the noir years and speaks about both the draw of the movies and the humiliation of attending movies as a black woman in the 1940s and 1950s. These individuals add vibrancy to the world of jazz and movie-going in the noir years.

In chapter 3, "Studio Jazz from Harlem to Acapulco," I consider how jazz works in *Out of the Past* (1947) and seek to discover how and why the working script changed from overtly racist in representing a Harlem jazz club to not at all racist in less than two weeks. I examine the production of the film, including the censorship files from the Production Code Administration. I also look specifically at Mexican sequences, in a cantina, a gambling establishment, and a bar, focusing on the attention paid to the portrayal of Mexican nationals, a type of representation explicitly controlled by the censors. In chapter 4, that examination of the treatment of race continues as I discuss the extended use of jazz and the jazz club sequence in *The Blue Gardenia* (1953) and the nuclear-noir *Kiss Me Deadly* (1953). I contrast those complex treatments with *Collateral* (2004), a neo-noir made and set in the present, which uses jazz as a generic noir feature and disempowers black artistry and jazz.

Next, I interpret various films noirs from the late 1950s whose jazz soundtracks were composed by working musicians, sometimes including appearances by those musicians on screen. I consider the narrative, the filmmakers, and the music, focusing especially on how jazz affects the film. Chapter 5 explores how Chico Hamilton and Fred Katz of the Chico Hamilton Quintet scored the music for *Sweet Smell of Success* (1957). Their contributions were replaced by music composed by Elmer Bernstein; however, the Hamilton Quintet appears on screen, and fortunately some of their compositions do make it onto the soundtrack. Chapter 6 discusses Miles Davis, composer of one of the first complete jazz soundtracks for a film noir. Unlike the other films discussed here, *Elevator to the Gallows* (1957) is French. Davis often turns up on soundtracks, as he does in *Collateral*, where the jazz legend is a plot point, but here Davis composes a full score. Ever the innovator, he also uses the cinematic assignment to explore a new interest in modal music, pursuing his own artistic agenda within the confines of the film work. Here, as David Butler notes, jazz gains an association with the "privileged non-diegetic space."[8] This privileging—providing music not specifically connected with the sight of a band or musician and therefore capable of abstract commentary and improvisation—changed how jazz worked in film.

Once composer and innovator Davis had composed a complete soundtrack for a film that had solid commercial success, Ellington and his collaborator Strayhorn managed to land a composing gig for Otto Preminger in *Anatomy of a Murder*. This is explored in chapter 7, " 'All the Very Gay Places': Ellington and Strayhorn Swing in Northern Michigan." Although a courtroom drama, *Anatomy* features murder, sex, and ambiguous motivations and morality. Ellington and Strayhorn's sophisticated and swinging sound supports the drama, occasionally commenting overtly, but mostly providing subtle and complex observations on the action. Jazz helps raise *Anatomy* to the level of film noir. In chapter 8, "Cannoy's Club: 'All Men Are Evil,'" I consider *Odds Against Tomorrow* (1959), a late classic noir that takes an overt but nuanced look at race and racism. The soundtrack is composed and conducted by John Lewis and features the Modern Jazz Quartet (MJQ), as well as other musicians. While the film is didactic, it offers moments of rare cinematic beauty and narrative sensitivity. The soundtrack adds emotional content, as Hollywood music usually does, but extends beyond the story to offer a searing commentary on the world the movie depicts. The Lewis score exemplifies how jazz allows and provides that level of abstract commentary.

Soon after, in the early 1960s, other forms and styles of music take over in Hollywood. But jazz still appears in film soundtracks occasionally, such as in the recent *American Hustle* (2014), which I discuss in the final chapter.

For me, *Odds Against Tomorrow, Anatomy of a Murder, Elevator to the Gallows*, and *Sweet Smell of Success* illustrate a vibrant and fleeting moment when Hollywood film noir and jazz made remarkable and unique meaning together, a moment when the primacy of the visual relinquished a measure of dominance to aural interpretations. Fleeger argues effectively that the aural potential of opera and jazz in early sound cinema always offered the possibility of active hearing to the spectator. I suspect that as the jazz and operatic voice fell away from common usage in early cinematic sound, so did the potential for spectators to hear the music as separate from the narrative. The sound of jazz in late classic noir might reactivate a sense of "connections both within and outside the text" for the spectator.[9] Before we get to those films, a historical look at jazz in film noir and jazz and movies in Utah starts this exploration.

CHAPTER ONE

Pie Eye's Juke Joint

JAZZ AND ITS INTERPRETATIONS

Then you came along with your siren song
To temp me to madness.

MUSIC AND LYRICS BY BILLY STRAYHORN[1]

Imagine a new kind of active spectator, one encouraged to draw
connections both within and outside of the text that are not entirely
directed by the narrative trajectory of the film or its music.

JENNIFER FLEEGER, *SOUNDING AMERICAN:*
HOLLYWOOD, OPERA, AND JAZZ[2]

ABOUT HALFWAY THROUGH *ANATOMY OF A MURDER* (1959), the protagonist, a small-town lawyer (James Stewart), politely but firmly removes his client's sexy wife (Lee Remick) from a roadhouse where she is drinking and dancing with male friends. Outside the bar, the lawyer attempts to regulate the young woman's behavior while black jazzmen play on in the background, audible and visible through a plate-glass window. He tells her, "Now you listen to me. Until this trial is over, you're gonna be a meek little housewife with horn-rimmed spectacles, and you're gonna stay away from men and juke joints and booze and pinball machines and you're gonna wear a skirt and low-heeled shoes, and you're gonna wear a girdle, and especially a girdle." She is not to tempt any man to madness, or any more men.

Anatomy of a Murder features a soundtrack composed by Duke Ellington and Billy Strayhorn. Although primarily a courtroom drama, coming out as classic film noir was waning, the film epitomized the way a few late

FIGURE 1.1. *The regulation of female behavior* (Anatomy of a Murder, *1959)*

classic noirs featured music as both background sound and as jazz. The jazz stood apart from the narrative and developed other ways of making meaning audible. The above sequence illustrates one of the primary and stereotypical meanings of jazz in film noir: jazz is black, and black is subversive and threatening to white male order. During and after World War II, these existentially dark movies reflected the threats to masculinity lurking on the home front for many returning veterans, threats embodied in an ungirdled woman found drinking in juke joints, who played on male susceptibility to gain her advantage.

A style of filmmaking that included spectacular black-and-white cinematography with low-key lighting—dark shadows pierced through with shards of light—film noir had narratives that also obscured motivations and desires, often featuring a flashback structure and voice-over. No one clearly wins; everyone loses something. Many noirs have features one might see as generic—the hard-boiled, tough-talking detective; the seductive, dangerous femme fatale; and the urban streets slicked with rain, as in *The Maltese Falcon* (1941), *Out of the Past* (1946), and *The Big Sleep* (1946). In classic film noir, the femme fatale represents a definitive threat to the men she seduces and, therefore, to male spectators. For female spectators, she represents freedom and agency, although, thanks to industry censors, her desires could never remain unchecked; she has to wind up dead, in jail, or married—with any luck to Humphrey Bogart.[3]

Despite its intimate association with the detective film, film-noir style is transgeneric and includes women's films and melodramas such as *Mildred Pierce* (1945), westerns such as *Johnny Guitar* (1954) and *High Noon*

(1952), and male melodramas such as *The Bigamist* and *The Hitch-Hiker* (both 1953).

Classic film noir begins with *The Maltese Falcon*—which featured the hard-boiled detective, femme fatale, and criminals, urbane and otherwise—and *Citizen Kane* (1941), which ushered in the complex narrative style and much of the camera work, lighting, and mise-en-scène that became typical of the style: the low-key lighting suggesting obscured motivations and morality, the off-angle compositions implying a world out of balance, and the strangely cavernous small spaces evoking a trap or noose. *Touch of Evil*, another film by Welles from 1958, signals the demise of the hard-boiled detective operating according to his own code of ethics in the obese and immoral police detective Quinlen (Welles). Extreme camera angles, relentless close-ups, rape, drugs, human trafficking, and murder of friends and enemies all imply the world of noir has sunk as low as it can.

Anatomy of a Murder comments and reflects on classic film noir right as the style itself is replaced by color and other cinematic interests. As with the detective and femme fatale, juke joints often appear in noir narratives, and *Anatomy of a Murder* is no exception. These smoky clubs uniformly represent the dangers of otherness, of erotic desires and deadly femininity, of uncontrollable urges leading to destruction. It is why the lawyer drags the woman out to deliver a conservative lecture, and it is why the camera shot includes jazzmen in the background rather than framing the two principals in a medium close-up. *Anatomy of a Murder* draws on earlier films noirs. For instance, in *Phantom Lady* (1944), a woman (Ella Raines) urges a musician (Elisha Cook Jr.) into an orgiastic drum solo during an after-hours jam session in a jazz cellar. In *Out of the Past* a detective's (Robert Mitchum) descent into the arms of the femme fatale (Jane Greer) and his eventual demise begins in a Harlem jazz club. An accountant's (Edmond O'Brien) night out in *D.O.A.* (1950) includes a San Francisco club, with a hot and raucous black band playing, in which he is fatally poisoned. He spends the rest of the movie seeking his own murderer. The lesson in all these films is that the jazz musician, the jazz club, and the music are licentious and uncontained and will lead to trouble of the deadliest sort. The lesson was so powerful that jazz still retains an association with the films of the noir years, the early 1940s to the late 1950s, even though music played by jazz musicians relatively rarely graces the soundtracks of the films.

That association of jazz, sex, and danger persists in Hollywood film and television. Hollywood produced classic films noirs during a mutable time for the industry. The style had its genesis in the early 1940s, when the classical Hollywood system dominated and émigré European film art-

FIGURE 1.2.
The urging
(Phantom Lady, *1944*)

FIGURE 1.3.
And the urged
(Phantom Lady, *1944*)

FIGURE 1.4.
The dangerous jazz club
(D.O.A., *1950*)

ists, directors, cinematographers, and editors bolstered the look of American films. Hollywood experienced the dismantling of the system with the Paramount antitrust case of 1948, leading to a US Supreme Court decision that ended the block booking of films and studio-owned movie theaters, a development that allowed for the rise of independent producers. The early films were shaped by the industry censors, the Production Code Administration (PCA), yet noir directors, along with changing cultural attitudes, eventually disempowered the PCA. During this time, the country experienced two major wars, World War II (WWII) and the Korean War, and witnessed the devastating potential of nuclear weapons. The struggle of African Americans for civil rights was another sort of national crisis of conscience. Jazz, primarily the production of African Americans, served as the soundtrack for the noir years, if not films noirs. Swing music, adopted by white musicians and and adapted to popular tastes, played on the radio and in every dance hall. By the mid-1940s, bebop expressed both technical expertise and black dissatisfaction with how jazz had entered the white mainstream. All these currents are expressed in classic film noir.

When I discuss jazz in film noir here, I look for jazz musicians performing, composing, or miming jazz on screen. I do not include jazz-inflected scores, such as Alex North's *A Streetcar Named Desire* (1951). I do not include Elmer Bernstein's score for *The Man with the Golden Arm* (1953), although the appearance of Shorty Rogers and Shelly Manne would count. I do not dispute the superb contributions of composers such as Bernstein and North, both of whom, according to Mervyn Cooke, "were motivated by a combination of nationalism [jazz as a uniquely American idiom], modernism, and an awareness of the deep-seated emotive and associative power of jazz."[4] Jazz composed and played by jazz musicians appears in classic film noir occasionally, but not nearly as often as it is associated with the mood of the films in retrospect. This association comes from both the stereotypical use of vaguely or overtly jazzy music and settings to signal danger, destruction, sexual promiscuity, and drug use in Hollywood movies, as well as the integration of those stereotypes into more sophisticated and modern movie scoring practices in the 1950s.

In the 1940s and 1950s, when social activists insisted African Americans appear in movies as something other than stereotypes, nightclub scenes also provided the perfect means for Hollywood to circumvent a problem it did not have the will to solve. Thomas Cripps notes that in 1942 Walter White, head of the National Association for the Advancement of Colored People (NAACP), engaged in a comprehensive campaign to "broaden the roles in which Negroes were pictured."[5] White told Joseph Breen, head of the PCA, that "the matter of the treatment of the Negro in motion picture" is of great importance to us.[6] Anna Everett suggests that better treatment of blacks in terms of representation resulted in fewer and fewer roles. In 1947, black critic Robert Jones pointed out that "the solution to protests against stereotyping the Negro has been quite simple for Hollywood; cut them altogether."[7]

If they were not left out altogether, black women in cinematic nightclubs become singers and chic patrons instead of cooks or mammies, and black men become musicians and sophisticated, well-dressed customers instead of porters or servants, although many still worked as waiters or bartenders on screen. The nightclub also provided a venue for popular jazz entertainers such as Ellington, Nat King Cole, Louis Armstrong, and Hazel Scott, who could perform in these locales without directly affecting the filmic narrative. As Donald Bogle points out, these sequences could be inserted to capitalize on the black entertainers and were often "cut from the films . . . should local (or Southern) theater owners feel their audience would object to seeing a Negro."[8] Even when the black entertainer or bit player made it onto the screen, Southern distributors freely cut scenes that portrayed blacks less stereotypically, despite ongoing pressure from activists.[9]

In the 1940s, blacks were mostly confined to bit parts, in the background or in brief nightclub sequences, although thanks to social pressures, the roles were somewhat less stereotypical. By the 1950s, as Anna Everett points out, "Sidney Poitier, Harry Belafonte, Dorothy Dandridge, Ruby Dee, and Ethel Waters were box office draws for black and white audiences."[10] I discuss Harry Belafonte's outing as producer and star of *Odds Against Tomorrow* in chapter 8.

In some films noirs, the night club scene might not be as easily cut. Vivian Sobchack notes that these movies regularly featured "salon spaces— nightclubs, cocktail lounges, and bars"—as a primary setting, spaces she interprets as "a perverse and dark response to the loss of a home."[11] In *Dames in the Driver's Seat*, I problematize Sobchack's reading.[12] The nightclub in film noir represents danger, seduction, and destruction, but at the same time, it often enhances the characterization of the white male protagonist and portrays a vibrant and positive black culture as well. In films noirs, the brief black jazz club sequences are often integral to the plot. While still providing entertainment for the spectator, the scenes also yield crucial information (or misinformation) for the hard-boiled white protagonist and serve to prefigure some impending threat to him or to bolster his outsider status and thereby his hip white masculinity. Early in my thinking about film noir, I redefined the term femme fatale to indicate her own demise, which she usually orchestrates just as effectively as she does the demise of any man, and renamed her opposing archetype, the woman as redeemer, femme attrapée (or woman trapped by the patriarchy).[13] My goal was to displace masculinity from its central position in the critical history of film noir. Might a similar move be made for the even more marginalized images of black nightclub patrons and jazz musicians in film noir?

Just as the nightclub sequence might be cut from some films, the historical and biographical information regarding these actors and scenes has been left out of much of film noir and Hollywood scholarship. David Butler's *Jazz Noir: Listening to Music from* Phantom Lady *to* The Last Seduction, and recent considerations, including Robert Miklitsch's *Siren City: Sound and Source Music in Classic American Noir* and Sheri Chinen Biesen's *Music in the Shadows: Noir Musical Films*, pay much needed attention to music in these films.[14] Here, I consider especially the club sequences and the soundtracks composed by working jazz composers to help make the changing social landscape of the noir years audible.

In addition to Hollywood, other industries saw similar demands for social justice. Eric Lott details the growing militancy among black Ford Motor Company workers and black officers and soldiers who fought in World War II.[15] The "double V" (for victory) campaign was promoted by the African American newspaper the *Pittsburgh Courier*, beginning early in 1942 through 1943, and also supported by other black newspapers. Said one black veteran of the fight at home: "I spent four years in the army to free a bunch of Dutchmen and Frenchmen, and I'm hanged if I'm going to let an Alabama version of the Germans kick me around when I get home."[16] Not surprisingly, many black musicians refused to serve in the military, and blacks made up about a third of those who failed to report when drafted to serve in the armed forces.[17]

African Americans and the country gained an awareness of black dissatisfaction with the status quo, expressed through protests, for example, among black railroad workers over racial bias in the military and race riots in larger cities in the early 1940s. For many black musicians this political consciousness was expressed in the shift from swing to bebop in the mid-1940s.[18] Bebop, according to Arthur Knight, "marked a change in jazz from mainstream popular music to an explicit art music, which was (at least initially) assertively black and (at least nascently) cultural-nationalist."[19] Knight, Scott DeVeaux, Lott, and others note that the turmoil surrounding the bebop revolution reflected black cultural and political "militancy of the moment," with "the music attempt[ing] to solve at the level of style what the militancy fought out in the streets."[20] Although bebop is often portrayed as anti-commercial, DeVeaux argues that bebop instead changed how the musicians and the audience related. Bebop artists offered their compositions and innovations more for appreciative listeners than dancers, and thereby avoided "the most debilitating or distasteful consequences of the [racist] cash nexus" that supported jazz.[21] Bebop, consciously black and intentionally different from swing and New-Orleans-style jazz, provided a militant soundtrack for the 1940s and 1950s. At the same time, radio provided a wide audience with access to swing and, for the more sophisticated listener, to bebop. Of course, the anonymity of the airwaves somewhat separated the listeners from the potential militancy of the musicians.

Hollywood style, dominated by capitalism, is also anti-militant, but the nightclubs of film noir provide a setting for both what Knight calls the "segregated look of swing" and the "'authentic' black invention" of bebop."[22] In many noirs, the white protagonists work in nightclubs as singers, dancers, or musicians. Examples include Veronica Lake's character in *This Gun for Hire* (1942), June Vincent's and Dan Duryea's characters in *Black Angel* (1946), and Ida Lupino's character in *Road House* (1948). In other noirs, the white male protagonist visits a jazz club where he is the only white person there; the musicians, singers, and other patrons are all African American. In later noirs, such as *Anatomy of a Murder*, the juke joint directly implies danger even as the jazz soundtrack points forward to more positive aspirations for a uniquely American music, albeit within the confines of Hollywood style.

In most interpretations of classical Hollywood film, including films noirs, the musical score is subordinated to the image, and both serve the narrative. Claudia Gorbman writes that music in these films serves to grease "the wheels of the cinematic pleasure machine by easing the spectator's passage into subjectivity . . . bidding the spectator to believe, focus, behold, identify, consume."[23] Gorbman provides a detailed discussion of neo-Marxist theorists Hanns Eisler and Theodor Adorno's critique of classical Hollywood scoring practices in their *Composing for Film* (1947). As Gorbman details, for Eisler and Adorno, Hollywood uses music solely to aid and abet the culture industry, eliminating the possibility of social activism.[24] A product of the Hollywood system, film noir music fits these parameters. For me, jazz in film noir adds another element to the system, an element that Jennifer Fleeger suggests occurs in sound film from the earliest days, one that encourages "connections both within and outside of the text that are not entirely directed by the narrative trajectory of the film."[25]

As I have shown, early in film noir, jazz serves as a trope for the seduction and danger stereotypically associated with the urban realm and otherness, an illusion of reality evoked by just the sound of a saxophone. For example, the jazz sequence in *D.O.A.* opens with a close-up on a poster of a black saxophone player. A live musician (James E. Streeter) steps into the shot, blowing furiously. As the camera pulls out, the rest of the quintet appear, the word "jive" on a fisherman's float behind them (see figure 1.4).[26] The white male protagonist is clearly uncomfortable, telling an attractive blonde enjoying the music at the bar that he can live without jazz music, just after he sips his poisoned bourbon. Here, as Kathryn Kalinak writes, the jazz works stereotypically, as a sort of leitmotif for "otherness," for "the urban, the sexual, and the decadent in a musical idiom perceived in the culture at large as an indigenous black form."[27]

David Butler's *Jazz Noir* provides a superb overview of film noir, film music, and jazz, including a detailed discussion of films from the 1940s and 1950s and a discussion of jazz in contemporary noir films. As Butler notes, "the tendency in film noir, and Hollywood in general, in the 1940s [was] to portray the sexual, rhythmic, impulsive aspects of jazz (the very aspects upon which the white culture industry mythologized jazz as dark, exotic, forbidden music)."[28] He argues this portrayal contrasted starkly with the bebop style of a new generation of musicians rising to prominence in the mid-1940s.[29] Butler also notes that despite the association in our cultural imagination of jazz and film noir, almost no modern jazz, or bebop, made it onto the screen during the 1940s.[30] In the 1950s, noir often featured jazz-inflected scores by Hollywood. Jazz in film now became a feature of the nondiegetic score, not exclusively emanating from the world of the film, such as the saxophone player in a club, but instead motivated by an internal logic of character or narrative.[31] Later, as working jazz musicians such as Chico Hamilton, John Lewis, Miles Davis, or Ellington and Strayhorn composed part or all of the nondiegetic score, jazz both served the Hollywood system's stereotypes and provided a nuanced and expanded contribution to filmic meaning, just as it meant more to the musicians themselves.

If jazz signified otherness for whites, for blacks it functioned in a wholly different way. African Americans, as DeVeaux points out, had seen "the profession of musician [take] its place alongside barber, caterer, and Pullman porter as one of the handful of occupations outside unskilled manual labor open to blacks."[32] DeVeaux cites a 1975 essay by Neil Leonard from the *Journal of Jazz Studies* suggesting that much like the Beat poets, "(w)hite musicians were . . . likely to take on the role of 'jazzman as romantic outsider,' becoming artists as an expression of their contempt for middle-class culture," while for blacks "the music profession offered one of the few consistent means of social advancement."[33] Utah jazzman Joe McQueen provides a fascinating glimpse into jazz as a means of personal and social progress. Nat King Cole also capitalized on his popularity with film performances in absentia and in person. Chico Hamilton took his West Coast cool to the streets of New York City; Miles Davis filled out his Paris nightclub work with a soundtrack for young Louis Malle's first solo film; Ellington and Strayhorn sought acceptance into Hollywood music-making; and John Lewis brought the Modern Jazz Quartet into full contact with the process of scoring a film. These were working musicians with musical agendas that reached far beyond the Hollywood system, yet these men also wanted the financial and commercial success that Hollywood promised.

For these jazz musicians, the music came first, but film provided more access to wider audiences and new venues to spin their expertise into gold. They were not the only ones to profit. I suggest that the jazz created by working jazz musicians for Hollywood film soundtracks in the late 1950s enhanced the filmic narratives (aesthetic profit) and also functioned as something else altogether, a disruptive hint about the world beyond the one Hollywood portrayed (societal profit). Film music helps maintain the illusion of a seamless and pleasurable reality for the spectator, but jazz also points more directly to the means of production, especially when the film includes the musicians nominally producing or even composing the sound. So jazz functions as both a stereotypical signifier of otherness and as something more than that, especially in the late 1950s.

Some theorists, such as Christopher Coady and Jeffrey Magee, identify jazz's ability to function within the Hollywood musical system and simultaneously offer a disruption or addition to that system as Afro-modernist subversion. Coady, drawing on Houston Baker, defines Afro-modernism as "an ideology in which discursive strategies from outside the African-American cultural set are used during the act of advancing African-American presence," and sees John Lewis "utilizing the veneer of hegemonic alignment as a vehicle for vernacular promotion" of his musical goals.[34] This "hegemonic alignment" with the needs of the Hollywood soundtrack, at the same time as jazz composers such as Davis, Ellington, and Lewis pursued their own musical and commercial successes, seems to work in multiple registers: the world of the film, the world of jazz, and the commercial world which measures artistic output in economic terms. Magee suggests "Afro-Modernism manifests itself in efforts to blend or juxtapose the earthy and the urbane, the down-home and the cosmopolitan, the simple and the sophisticated," and sees the "chief musical conduit of Afro-Modernism . . . [as] the blues."[35]

The jazz musicians who compose for films noirs in the late 1950s, including Chico Hamilton and Fred Katz, Ellington and Strayhorn, Davis, and Lewis, blend European classical music traditions with jazz and blues, including improvisation. Their work integrates, with varying levels of success, popular movie traditions and jazz artistry, asking spectators to listen, watch, and perhaps hear things differently. In discussing Lewis's ability to seamlessly synthesize jazz and blues idioms with classical modes, Coady speculates that Lewis provided a pleasurable experience for both the neophyte and musically sophisticated listeners.[36] The entertainment and recruitment functions of jazz provide an explanation for how the music seems to work in film noir in the late 1950s and relate to Fleeger's thesis about opera and jazz in early sound film. Those who knew the music listened for and understood the complexities of the soundtrack, knowing that it worked otherwise than typical film music. The spectator who did not know the music also experienced an unfamiliar disconnect between the images on screen and the accompanying music, a disconnect that compelled more attention to music in classic film noir than movies usually required.

Jazz in late classic film noir certainly signifies it is dialogical, functioning within the accepted discourses of Hollywood and Hollywood-influenced film culture, in jazz, classical, blues, and other musical traditions, and in the social context of race and class. In his autobiography, Ellington points precisely to the necessity of a double consciousness, of communicating on multiple levels, when he suggests, "having a story to go with what you were going to play was of vital importance. . . . The audience didn't know anything about it, but the cats in the band did."[37] Afromodernism, the intentional blending of various musical traditions and tropes with jazz, calls attention to the momentary disruption of the primacy of the visual that allows jazz to be heard at the movies and suggests an agenda in the jazz community to explain the intentionality of the disruption.

Having studied German literature, I also see an alienation effect in jazz's ability to take its place as Hollywood-appropriate music and to speak to other audiences and goals. Bertolt Brecht provides a description of what he identifies as the alienation effect (*Verfremdungseffekt*) on stage in his 1948 "A Short Organum for the Theater."[38] Brecht suggests that "the theater must alienate what it shows."[39] He continues, "In order to produce a-effects," or alienation effects, "the actor no longer has to persuade the audience that it is the author's character and not himself that is standing on the stage."[40] When it comes to music, Brecht argues that, for the desired alienation effect to occur, "music must strongly resist the smooth incorporation which is generally expected of it and turns it into an unthinking slavey [*sic*]; Music does not 'accompany' except in the form of comment."[41] Instead, "music can make its point in a number of ways with full independence, and can react in its own manner to the subjects dealt with; at the same time it can also quite simply help to lend variety to the entertainment."[42] A Marxist like Eisler and Adorno, Brecht argues for a theater that arouses attention and potentially leads to social action and engagement rather than numbing or deadening the spectator to that potential. I contend that the use of jazz in a film soundtrack produces an alienation effect, making the familiar slightly less legible. In the films I discuss here, some element of the jazz—a single note played by a black horn player, a sequence in a jazz club that provides unexpected information about the white protagonist, jazz taking its place as nondiegetic music, or as both diegetic and nondiegetic—disrupts Hollywood's seemingly smooth incorporation of music and even works toward other agendas.

This seems especially true in the films noirs made in the mid to late 1950s, when the use of jazz and the sight of black musicians and composers on screen acting as themselves could shock the spectator out of the complacency usually created by classical Hollywood soundtracks. Hollywood used jazz to represent otherness, danger, sexuality, femininity, and the threat of urban spaces. Jazz music served as the soundtrack to the 1940s and 1950s, playing in dance halls, on the radio, and, by the end of the period, in concert halls such as Carnegie Hall and concert formats such as the Jazz at the Philharmonic series from 1944–1957. The popularity of the music and the liberal bent of the directors and producers of films noirs led to the use of jazz composers and musicians. The presence of the artistic, productive other on screen and behind the scenes implicitly embedded black activism into the primarily white output of Hollywood and changed how music affected the filmic narrative. When the musicians appear on screen, the spectator's abstract awareness of film music necessarily becomes more concrete. Laura Mulvey, considering melodrama, suggests that "the amount of dust the story raises along the road, a cloud of overdetermined irreconcilables which put up resistance to being neatly settled in the last five minutes of the film," makes things interesting.[43] Jazz adds a dusting of complexity to Hollywood films noirs, and the additional presence of the jazz musician in the film ensures the complexity cannot be ignored. Jazz soundtracks, composed by working jazz musicians, introduce a measure of dissonance. Fleeger sees this as part of what jazz in the cinema has always done; Coady and Magee see this as Afromodernist subversion. I see it as an alienation effect. We are all pointing to a similar event in cinema spectatorship: the experience of jazz as both a classical Hollywood soundtrack and a primarily African American aspirational cultural discourse. Jazz encourages the spectator to hear a movie explicitly, and sometimes, in the 1940s and 1950s, to see African Americans on screen explicitly, not usually a part of Hollywood film-going experiences. For my purposes, Afromodernism relates to how the jazz artists work with music in classic film noir; the alienation effect relates more generally to how jazz functions in classic film noir.

Before we go to the movies and start considering those effects, we visit the Porters and Waiters Club in Ogden, Utah.

CHAPTER TWO

The Porters and Waiters Club

JAZZ, MOVIES, AND OGDEN

*I*N 2005, AS A RECENT TRANSPLANT TO UTAH ALREADY devoted to jazz, I read with great interest an article by Brandon Griggs in the *Salt Lake Tribune* with the headline "Jazzman happy to call Utah home," about a local musician, a saxophonist who had lived in Ogden, Utah, since the mid-1940s.[1] The article detailed Ogden's thriving midcentury jazz scene, noting that Nat King Cole, Count Basie, Ellington, and bebop innovators Charlie Parker and Dizzy Gillespie had all come through town on the train. They stopped and played with the local musician, a gentleman named Joe McQueen, at a venue devoted to African American patrons. The Porters and Waiters Club, on 25th Street, near Union Station, gave my research project—examining jazz in classic films noirs—a new direction. McQueen, a black jazz musician and social activist, played and lived through the swing-to-bebop transition, a musical revolution that reflected black political and social activism that made it, indirectly, onto Hollywood screens in the jazz sequences in films noirs. As I researched the city, I met Betty Moore, granddaughter of slaves and cousin of jazzman Art Farmer, who was born and raised in the town and an avid movie fan as well. Moore was a young black woman in the turbulent 1940s and 1950s. She listened to jazz at home and in clubs, and was a regular moviegoer. McQueen and Moore agreed to talk with me and brought to life the struggles represented obliquely in film noir with their first-person accounts; they and the Porters and Waiters Club provide connections to jazz and film noir directly from Utah.

Originally settled in 1847 by members of the Church of Jesus Christ of Latter-Day Saints (LDS), today Utah is the most conservative and one of the least diverse states in the United States, but Ogden is not a typical Utah town. Census data from 2013 reports the population of Utah is 91.6

percent white, while the US is 77.7 percent white. The US is 13.2 percent black, while Utah is 1.3 percent black. Ogden, however, has almost twice that black population, 2.2 percent.[2] As a major railroad town since the 1870s, Ogden was nicknamed the "Junction City." As Richard Roberts details, Ogden was more diverse than the rest of the state and one of the few places in Utah where LDS, or Mormon, leadership was contested in the late nineteenth century, leading to the election of a non-Mormon, a Gentile according to LDS terminology, as mayor in 1889.[3] The construction of Hill Air Force Base in 1938 and then World War II renewed Ogden's significance "as a transportation hub and center of government agencies and war industries."[4] At that time, the south side of 25th Street, leading directly into town from Union Station, housed many black-owned businesses including the Royal Hotel and the Porters and Waiters Club; both served black rail workers and travelers.

Originally called the Railroad Porters and Waiters Club, later shortened to the Porters and Waiters Club, the establishment was started by William "Billy" Weakley in 1912, according to Mark Zoellner.[5] The club offered sleeping accommodations, a pool hall, and a cafe to black railroad workers. In his memoirs, Frank Marshall Davis, a black journalist and poet, recalls staying at the club in the mid-1920s when he was first hired as a waiter by Union Pacific.[6] He notes the club "was a drag unless you drank, shot pool, or gambled."[7] In the mid-1940s, the club owner, Weakley, married a young woman named Anna Belle Shaw, who "in short order whipped his establishment into a model of efficiency."[8] A downstairs jazz venue was added, and the club hosted Mel Torme and the Four Freshmen, with drop-in visits from artists such as Ellington and Charlie Parker, according to a *Salt Lake Tribune* article detailing Utah's jazz history by Eileen Stone.[9] The Porters and Waiters Club linked both the opportunities and the social inequities experienced by African Americans. The club provided for the influx of black military men and their families and for railroad workers. It offered a place to eat, sleep, and recreate to blacks. In the 1950s, whites also enjoyed the entertainment of jazz at the Porters and Waiters Club.

Although Ogden's history was a surprise to me, the town was apparently known to hipsters in the mid-twentieth century. In Jack Kerouac's *On the Road*, just a few pages into his trip across the country, Sal Paradise hitches a ride with other travelers on a flatbed truck. Sal meets fellow vagabond Montana Gene, who tells Sal he must stop in Ogden, saying, "It's the place where most of the boys pass thru and always meet there; you're liable to see anybody there."[10] In the 1940s and 1950s, the mostly middle-class, white Beats aspired to the hipness they saw embodied in

FIGURE 2.1.
The Royal Hotel in
2005 (Author's photo)

FIGURE 2.2.
A holiday glass
from the Porters
and Waiters Club
(Glass courtesy of
Ogden Union Station
Archive [OUSA];
author's photo)

FIGURE 2.3. *Anna Belle and William "Billy" Weakley, owners of the Porters and Waiters Club (Courtesy of OUSA)*

blacks; for African Americans, aspirations were different. In Ogden, the railroad provided employment for black residents as cooks, waiters, servers, porters, and in businesses catering to those workers, such as the Porters and Waiters Club. Otherwise, in California, for example, bit parts in Hollywood movies, careers in the defense and service industries, including the railroads, and careers as jazz musicians provided blacks with the possibility of entry into the American middle class. As jazz filled the airways in the 1940s and 1950s, even in Utah, race counted in the motivation for becoming a musician.

Radio served as the primary means to expose listeners outside major metropolitan areas to jazz. Laurence M. Yorgason writes about jazz on AM radio in Utah from 1945 until 1964, looking at radio station logs and newspapers from the period.[11] Yorgason concludes that, although "early radio broadcasts of jazz in Utah came by way of hookups to live performances from distant big cities," by the late 1940s, "local remote broadcasts featured both Utah and celebrity swing bands" at a number of popular dance venues along the Wasatch Front, the urban centers located on the western slope of the Wasatch Mountain range.[12] Yorgason focuses on various jazz DJs, beginning with Al Collins, a Chicago transplant who started jazz programming in 1945 and worked until 1957, playing mainly swing. During those years, he saw his time slot move from early evening prime time to late night.[13] After Collins, the white disk jockeys "focused their appeal on a more 'sophisticated' listening audience: the white connoisseurs of jazz."[14] As it did across the country, regular jazz radio programming became scarce as other types of music became more popular in the mid-1960s. Yorgason concludes by noting that today only one station had a regular late night jazz program.[15] Sadly, for those of us driving home at night in Utah, that radio show ended with the retirement of Steve Williams, a Utah jazz disk jockey, in 2015.

McQueen came to Utah right as swing was becoming popular, even in rural midwestern states, through the medium of radio. Yorgason does

FIGURE 2.4. *Cooks in the kitchen* (*Courtesy of* OUSA)

FIGURE 2.5. *Waiters and servers* (*Courtesy of* OUSA)

FIGURE 2.6.
Waiter serving coffee
(*Courtesy of* OUSA)

FIGURE 2.7.
Red caps, or porters
(*Courtesy of* OUSA)

not discuss local jazz musicians, but it seems likely that McQueen worked some of those radio broadcasts. McQueen took advantage of the opportunity for social advancement offered by jazz. He was an avid athlete as a young man but realized he could not make money with those skills. He relates how his cousin, Hershel Evans, who played in Count Basie's Orchestra, came to visit his family and told McQueen to "start playing horn" to earn a living. McQueen picked up the horn (he went through the clarinet and tuba before arriving at the saxophone) and has been playing ever since. He wound up in Utah in 1945, when his band leader gambled away their pay. According to McQueen, Ogden was no worse than any other place, and the black-owned restaurants and clubs on 25th Street made it seem better than some. He worked various jobs—at the railroad station as a red cap, or baggage handler, at nearby Hill Air Force Base as an auto mechanic, and at the pool hall in the Porters and Waiters Club—but throughout his life, he played jazz.

Charlie Parker, who along with Dizzy Gillespie and Bud Powell created bebop, came though Ogden just as bebop exploded onto the jazz scene. McQueen could not recall the date but talks about playing *Now's the Time*, a bebop classic, with Parker one night in Ogden. Richard Seidel helps provide a possible date; he suggests the tune was from Parker's "very first studio session as a leader in 1945 for Savoy."[16] McQueen reminisces:

> Yeah, so he [Parker] had just written the tune when he came through here. He was on his way to California, and he stopped at a club down here where I was playing . . . and there was another guy named Malone on the door . . . Malone didn't know who he was, and so he [Parker] said, "Hey man, go get that saxophone player. Tell him to come down here." So I got down there and my mouth fell open! . . . So I got him on in there . . . pretty soon he said "Hey, man, I wrote this little ditty here. Say, I want to show you this thing here. You might like it, you know." And I played it with him right after he wrote it and play it all the time now.

The militancy of bebop rode through the country on the rails, arguably making it possible for McQueen to insist, only a few years later, that his black friends be allowed in to hear him play in white-owned and previously whites-only clubs. McQueen says when he landed in Ogden it "was a pretty prejudiced place . . . but there were so many black clubs and things here." Even the Porters and Waiters Club remained segregated, at least until 1954, according to Zoellner. McQueen tells me his band was so popular that the owners of whites-only clubs started to allow his friends

FIGURE 2.8.
McQueen as a young man (Courtesy of OUSA)

FIGURE 2.9.
McQueen's Casino Club band (Courtesy of OUSA)

and eventually anyone to come listen. He added, after a while "anywhere I played the people know right from the start that if they didn't let black people in, I wasn't going to be there." His confidence as a musician led to, and perhaps allowed, his social activism. He knew economics made his demands for social equity more powerful; if whites wanted to book his popular Casino Club band they had to let African Americans in the front door. Busy with gigs, jam sessions, and day jobs, McQueen was not a movie fan and tells me he went once or twice a month during the 1940s, if there was a show his wife wanted to see. Like many Americans, they stopped going to movies almost altogether with the advent of television. Betty Moore, however, was an avid moviegoer in the 1940s.

Ogden still has a beautiful restored movie palace, Peery's Egyptian Theater, which first opened in 1924. Five other movie theaters served the population in the 1940s and 1950s. Moore was let in the front door of the movie theaters but was then shuttled to the balcony or to one side of the auditorium. Moore detailed how movies were the "one outlet for entertainment. It was always humiliation to the human spirit to be directed to the balcony . . . one never, as a human being, becomes used to being humiliated. . . . You don't get hardened to it. You just suck it up and try to go on." To my surprise, when I asked how often she went to movies, she responded, "Once, sometimes twice a week." Moore's avid spectatorship, despite the humiliation she experienced, speaks to the powerful draw Hollywood movies exerted on consumers regardless of race.

As John Sedgwick points out, movies were "a most important twentieth-century commodity," and "in the years immediately following the end of the Second World War [film] consumption was confined to the movie theaters alone."[17] A cursory survey of the local Ogden paper, the *Standard Examiner*, between 1941 and 1958 reveals numerous movies we now identify as films noirs played in the local theaters. Sedgwick's research suggests that films categorized as drama, action-adventure, and crime made up a little over twenty-five percent of the top-grossing films at the time, and that "stars, and 'genre' served to differentiate the movie market."[18] For Moore, and for many consumers, stars provided images of consumer goods in the form of cigarettes, makeup, and clothes, and they also sold versions of gender relationships. Moore chose her movies based on the stars, naming Betty Davis, Joan Crawford, Janet Gaynor, and elaborated, "They all smoked, and looked so glamorous, and they painted their lips boldly. I loved to watch what they wore, how they walked, how they would just completely surrender themselves in a kiss." Moore's favorite stars, all white, represented another lack of choice she was faced with in consuming Hollywood movies, at least in the 1940s.

FIGURE 2.10. *Peery's Egyptian Theater in 1947 (Courtesy Van Summerill Collection)*

FIGURE 2.11. *Peery's Egyptian Theater in 2005 (Author's photo)*

FIGURE 2.12. *Image from Nov. 6, 1941, edition of the* Ogden Standard Examiner

The same year *The Maltese Falcon* screened in Ogden, the local news-paper, the *Ogden Standard Examiner* ran the above advertisement for Fol-gers Coffee.[19] It is the only representation of blacks I found in the paper. Moore subscribed to the *Examiner* for local news, although she also occa-sionally took the black newspaper, the *Chicago Defender,* or picked up an-other black paper, such as the *Pittsburgh Courier,* from someone travel-ing through town. Moore's pleasure in movie-going was mitigated by her treatment at the theaters and no doubt by what she saw on the screen. The newspaper advertisement perpetuates the same stereotypes about blacks that Hollywood promoted, and the jazz scenes in films are likewise no exception. Black film critic Lawrence Reddick's 1944 essay "Of Motion Pictures" presents the ways Hollywood reinforced black stereotypes, stat-ing "that the usual roles given to Negro actors call for types like Louise Beavers, Hattie McDaniel, 'Rochester,' Bill Robinson, Clarence Muse, and various Jazz musicians."[20]

However, despite the preponderance of stereotyped representations, the brief scenes containing blacks and jazz were contested sites, as my dis-cussion of *Out of the Past* in chapter 3 will make clear. And, in the war of representation, the "militancy of the moment," although filtered through the soft focus of the Hollywood production process, affected movies. As had been the case in Utah, jazz played a role in that change. The social history that produced bebop influenced, in a slight but marked way, how Hollywood represented jazz in film noir, resulting in portrayals of blacks that were less racist. McQueen and Moore lived through the tumultuous pre-civil-rights era in Ogden, a time when film noir, modernist jazz, swing, and bebop flourished in the United States. The Porters and Waiters Club, dependent on railroad business, closed its doors at the end of the 1950s, but before that, in 1954, it played a part in desegregating Ogden. Anna Belle Weakley Mattson says, "After they passed civil rights legisla-tion . . . we started letting a few white people come in downstairs to the lounge," men who ran white clubs on the Wasatch Front.[21] Music helped integrate a black club, just as the whites-only clubs allowed McQueen's friends and people to come hear him play.

Hollywood films noirs, made primarily by whites for a substantially white audience, afford an oblique historiography of jazz, a Hollywood-style map of musical, racial, and cultural tensions in black and white. The Folgers advertisement, McQueen's experiences as a black activist and jazz musician who played through the bebop revolution, and Moore's experiences as a moviegoer help to fill in some of the void left by Hollywood's version of jazz and cocktails during the classic film noir period, as does the Porters and Waiters Club, serving black customers and eventually white jazz fans. In the next few chapters, I will look at jazz and cocktail venues in Harlem and Acapulco in *Out of the Past* (1946) and then start to chart some of the changes Hollywood offers on the subject of jazz and African American representation in film noir.

CHAPTER THREE

Studio Jazz from Harlem to Acapulco

I thought for a while that your poignant smile
Was tinged with the sadness of a great love for me.

Ah yes! I was wrong,
Again I was wrong.

MUSIC AND LYRICS BY BILLY STRAYHORN[1]

R EPRESENTING A HOLLYWOOD VERSION OF OGDEN'S
Porters and Waiters Club, with its black employees, musi-
cians, and patrons, the Harlem jazz club in *Out of the Past* is a studio set.
The sequence opens with a phallic flourish, a close-up of a black horn-
player hitting a boisterous high note before moving into a dance groove.
Directed by Jacques Tourneur, based on the novel *Build My Gallows High*
by Daniel Mainwaring, the film's white male protagonist Jeff (Robert
Mitchum), while investigating femme fatale Kathie (Jane Greer), seeks
out her maid in the club. The black patrons remain oblivious to the white
interloper until Jeff gains an introduction to the maid, Eunice (Theresa
Harris), and her male companion (Caleb Peterson) via the headwaiter (the
uncredited Wesley Bly). After the opening notes, the trumpeter's tune becomes the love theme, "The First Time I Saw You," which is played over
the opening credits and associated exclusively with the protagonists' love
story, disappearing when they both die. Jeff is wrong about Kathie's love
for him, over and over, which leads directly to his demise.

In "The Vanishing Love Song in Film Noir," Krin Gabbard details the
use of the song and writes that the trumpeter is Gerald Wilson, "an important if underappreciated arranger and . . . leader of several well-regarded

jazz orchestras."[2] Wilson, who died in 2014 at the age of 97, was a vibrant part of the LA jazz scene. According to his obituary in the *LA Times*, he "provided arrangements and compositions for such major jazz artists as Duke Ellington, Dinah Washington, Billie Holiday, Sarah Vaughan, Dizzy Gillespie, Ella Fitzgerald, Nancy Wilson and others, as well as — from various genres — Bobby Darin, Harry Belafonte, B. B. King and Les McCann."[3] As Gabbard notes, the opening for the sequence breaks with standard Hollywood practice, which typically had musicians pretend to play using a prerecorded number, as in the jazz club in *D.O.A.*[4] Instead, Wilson actually seems to play the trumpet. The brief but "bracing, unaccompanied jazz cadenza" signifies something other than swing; for just a few seconds, bebop, played by a real jazzman, takes the screen.[5]

In this chapter, I consider the external pressures that shaped films noirs in the 1940s, including the Production Code Administration (PCA), which especially impacted the portrayal of the femme and homme fatal; the Office of War Information, which was concerned with black participation in the war effort and with the portrayal of the US abroad; and black activists, both musical and social. Called *Build My Gallows High* in the Radio-Keith-Orpheum (RKO) studio files, *Out of the Past*'s production history provides a useful model for considering other films noirs. The man who plays the headwaiter (see figure 3.2), Bly, has five roles listed in the Internet Movie Database (IMDb), three of them uncredited. In the 1950s, ten years after the campaign of the NAACP's Walter White to alter the stereotypes of African Americans in Hollywood, Bly plays a "timid native" in one film and a genie in another. The beautiful Eunice is played by Theresa Harris, a woman with over forty Hollywood movies on her filmography, including *Morocco* (1930), *Jezebel* (1938), *Cat People* (1942), and *Angel Face* (also with Mitchum, 1953). According to Ed Guerrero, Harris "found little work in the film industry after this part [in *Jezebel*] because she was 'too dark.'"[6] I do not fully understand that claim, since she worked in over twenty-eight films after 1938. Nevertheless, as Thomas Cripps points out, although Harris studied music at the University of Southern California, her roles were limited to maids and nurses.[7] Cripps adds that Harris and many other "*grandes dames* of the ghetto . . . gave without stint to help the race while at the same time supporting their style of life by playing traditional roles as domestic servants."[8] Eunice's male friend in *Out of the Past* has a similar professional biography.

Caleb Peterson was an accomplished bass baritone. According to Edward Mapp, he sang "Ol' Man River" on the soundtrack album of *Till the Clouds Roll By* (1947) and, like Harris, was consigned to bit parts in Hollywood (seven roles listed in IMDb).[9] While Harris devoted her time

FIGURE 3.1. *Trumpet player (Gerald Wilson) in Harlem jazz club*

FIGURE 3.2. *Eunice and her escort at the club*

and money to the local black community, Peterson became a vocal activist for African Americans, keeping White (of the NAACP) informed of Hollywood's intentions with regard to the portrayal of blacks during the 1940s so that White could exert pressure on the studios. Later Peterson went on to organize and head up the Hollywood Race Relations Bureau. According to the trade journal *Variety*, in 1962 after an arrest for picketing at the Academy Awards show, Peterson organized "the most massive attack yet on the Negro stereotype in American motion pictures . . . [using] the protest-and-pressure demonstration . . . via coast-to-coast picketing . . . at first-run theatres in some 60 key cities."[10] My point here is not to suggest that Peterson and Harris could have been famous, were it not for racism, although that is likely. Instead, I am interested in how their biographies inform the version of race relations presented in the film.

The dissonance of the opening trumpet chords in the jazz sequence imply confidence and even the phallic black militancy of bebop. As Gabbard explains, phallic horn elements include "spikes into the upper register, fast runs through a range of the instrument, and an often exaggerated feel for climaxes," and were used to express African American "masculinity at historical moments when other, comparable expressions were dangerous."[11] Here, the dangerous opening notes immediately mellow into a swinging refrain, withdrawing the phallic threat. The alienation effect of this moment, and the ensuing sequence, seems minimal, but it is there. Whites and blacks interact as social equals in the club; indeed, this is the only place they interact in the film. James Naremore suggests that Eunice "responds to Jeff's questions without a trace of subservience, all the while conveying a wry intelligence."[12] For Naremore, the whole scene "is played without condescension, and, whether it intends to or not, it makes a comment on racial segregation."[13] But like Jeff, who does not engage with black culture once he has gathered his information, white culture remains detached and uninterested in the racial struggle hinted at by the locale and music. Consequently, Jeff does not gain a great deal of patina from his exchanges with black culture here. He seems similarly laconic and detached, whether in a Mexican cafe or a New York jazz club.[14]

Perhaps that sense of detachment stems from Mitchum, the actor, more than from Jeff, the character. Robert Miklitsch compares Mitchum's underacting with Dizzy Gillespie, "who strategically underplays in cutting contests with younger, less experienced but overly ambitious musicians."[15] That does not explain it completely; Gillespie knew he would win the contest, while Jeff seems to know he cannot. For William Luhr, Mitchum's "performance gives Jeff a poetic complexity that often renders him more compelling and even sympathetic than the morally righteous characters."[16] I assert that this is always true of the femmes and hommes fatals, characters who resist the capitalist patriarchy through their excessive sexual and economic desires. These sexy characters' antisocial desires for money and sexual fulfillment must eventually be subject to Code-prescribed punishment for illegal and immoral behavior. Nevertheless, it is they who hold the spectator's interest, not the law-abiding femmes and hommes attrapés, characters who maintain the capitalist patriarchy through marriage and gainful employment.

That there were Code-prescribed punishments is historical fact. The Production Code Administration (PCA), led by Joseph Breen from 1934 until his retirement in 1954, and continuing until the 1960s, either granted or refused the seal of approval that allowed distribution and exhibition of a film. The scripts for films produced by the Hollywood studio system during the noir years were vetted by Breen, who was handpicked by the Catholic Legion of Decency to enforce the Production Code.[17] Geoffrey Shurlock, who spent years working with Breen and succeeded him as director of the PCA, noted the censors wanted the filmmakers to get it right, as they were "in the business of granting seals."[18]

However, audiences wanted filmmakers to get it right, too; meaning, they wanted provocative and alluring films despite and perhaps because of the constraints of censorship. And filmmakers did get it right. While censorship was universally resented by filmmakers, Stephen Weinberger documents the responses of various successful directors to Breen and the PCA's interventions; Weinberger quotes filmmaker John Huston who, "while absolutely opposed to censorship," said, "'no picture of mine was ever really damaged by censors . . . [as] there was usually a way around them.'"[19]

Censorship caused the script writers to write their way around and into the criminal and sexual lives of the protagonists. The femmes and hommes fatals' overt passions, criminality, and heedless attitude toward society's strictures that inevitably drove them to death and destruction—these all made for seductive cinema. At the same time, the Production Code insisted:

> That evil is not *presented alluringly*. Even if later in the film the evil is condemned or punished, it must not be allowed to appear so attractive that the audience's emotions are drawn to desire or approve as strongly that the later condemnation is forgotten and only the apparent joy of the sin is remembered.[20]

The Code does not define evil, but lumps "crime, wrong-doing, evil, and sin" in together, and it would certainly include criminal activities, adultery, sex outside of marriage, or what the Code calls "sex perversion," including obsession, as evils.[21] The corresponding pair to the femme and homme fatal, the femme and homme attrapé, do not remain untouched by evil but also do not engage in it.

The Code determined the outcomes for both sets of characters. The fatal ones through their destruction, and the trapped ones through their survival, uphold the moral imperative of the Code. No one, not even Burt Lancaster, could hold up an armored car without censure by a system that insisted crime "shall never be presented in such a way as to throw sympathy with the crime . . . or to inspire others with a desire for imitation."[22] No one, not even Jane Greer, could engage in passionate sex outside the bounds of marriage when the Code required that films "not infer that low forms of sex relationship are an accepted or common thing."[23] Even passionate sex within marriage was restricted, since "lustful kissing, lustful embraces, suggestive postures and gestures, are not to be shown," hence, the ubiquitous pair of single beds in the 1940s married couple's on-screen bedroom, and perhaps even the explosion that kills Bannion's (Glenn Ford) passionate wife in *The Big Heat* (1953).[24] The survival of femmes and hommes attrapés, the female and male redeemers, in film noir guaranteed the Code's general principle that "correct standards of life, subject only to the requirement of drama and entertainment, shall be presented."[25] These stringent restrictions should have prevented Hollywood from realistically portraying any timely social issues.

Yet by casting Burt Lancaster and Ava Gardner, Robert Mitchum and Jane Greer, or Jean Simmons as characters with dubious motivations, films noirs virtually assured the allure of the forbidden. The Code also dictated that "impure love must not be presented as attractive and beautiful."[26] In *The Killers* (1946), Gardner's character cheats on her husband with Swede, played by Lancaster. In *Angel Face* (1952), Simmons's character kills her beloved father in an attempt to murder her stepmother, and then kills her husband (Mitchum) and herself to ensure he not live without her. All this, while the femme and homme attrapé, those characters willing to live within society's rules, watch safely from the sidelines of the narrative. Despite their presence as stock characters, they do not enter the collective imagination. Perhaps this happens because most moviegoers lived lives much closer to those of the husband who works for a modest paycheck and the wife who wears herself out in the domestic economy, characters played by actors whose names almost no one remembers, such as Steve Brodie and Virginia Huston in *Out of the Past*, or Sam Levene and Vir-

FIGURE 3.3. *The femme and homme attrapé in* Out of the Past

ginia Christine in *The Killers*, or Mona Freeman and Kenneth Tobey in *Angel Face*.

Hollywood filmmakers and censors knew that people bought movie tickets to see the exciting, dangerous lives of desirous men and woman on screen. Sure, the couples who resembled the spectators survived the narrative, but briefly, cinematically, spectators could also identify with the forbidden on screen. They could hear it, too, in the jazz scores, a hint of anti-establishment music happening far away from their routine lives.

Other forces also impacted Hollywood output during and after World War II. Blacks had already experienced grave disappointment after they enthusiastically entered into the war effort in World War I, only to be faced with ongoing racist treatment in the military and at home. African American leader Adam Clayton Powell claimed, "Despite our apathy toward the war, it is not because we don't recognize the monster Hitler. . . . We recognize him immediately, because he is like minor Hitlers here. . . . The Gestapo is like the Ku Klux Klan here."[27] Clayton Koppes and Gregory Black interpret the *Pittsburgh Courier* "Double V" campaign as "an attempt by moderate black leaders to channel the anger of the black masses into safer bounds."[28] During World War II, the Office of War Information (owI), headed up by CBS radio personality Elmer Davis, contributed to film censorship, especially from 1942 through 1944.[29] And while film noir is generally identified as a post–World War II phenomenon, Sheri Chinen Biesen makes a convincing case for how "war-related circumstances, constraints, incentives, and the government's role in the media—and the film industry's effort to mobilize the war effort—culminated in a distinctly American national cinema" and produced film noir.[30] In fact, the Bureau of Motion Pictures set up shop in Hollywood to interact with the studios for the domestic branch of the OWI. Although its primary goal was to portray America positively at home and abroad, the OWI also concerned itself with getting blacks involved in the war effort, despite their reservations about fighting abroad.

Chinen Biesen also details some of the crucial social and industrial changes brought about by World War II. She mentions the lack of available film stock and the technological advancements in film that allowed filming in lower light situations, the actual blackouts imposed on nighttime Los Angeles, the influx of European and German directors, and the violence and suffering of the war captured and screened for movie audiences in newsreels. Chinen Biesen emphasizes the "profound variance between condoned, regulated, censored, and sanitized propaganda representation of the war and the realities of wartime culture."[31] These changes and others had an impact on noir films.

The OWI's Bureau of Motion Pictures eventually "sanctioned . . . violent depictions of (racial/Japanese atrocity) crime for war-related propaganda purposes," placing PCA strictures against screening violence in direct conflict with wartime propaganda requirements.[32] Chinen Biesen suggests these conflicts led to a relaxation of PCA standards in other areas; as the cultural climate became more hard-boiled and pessimistic, film noir did as well. Films noirs became more graphic in their representation of violence, and this realism also influenced how sexuality and criminality were presented on screen.

But the OWI's changes did little to help improve the representations of blacks in film, instead actually leading to fewer and fewer roles for blacks in Hollywood since it was easier to leave a black character out than rethink a black role. Relatively quickly, the OWI stopped worrying about how African Americans were represented in or responded to screen images, and instead it devoted its attention to the vision of American society exported abroad.[33] Hollywood did this by "having occasionally a 'Negro speak intelligently' and a 'sprinkling of average looking Negro people' in crowd scenes of bank-teller lines."[34] These images "of ordinary life . . . [promoted] an essentially false impression to the rest of the world: that blacks were full participants in American life."[35] For example, *The Mal-*

tese Falcon (1941) shows Sam Spade (Humphrey Bogart) walking past a black couple on a busy street as he carries the paper-wrapped falcon. War movies frequently showed the military as racially integrated during World War II when it would not actually be integrated until the Korean War.

No doubt these impressions also impacted how blacks viewed themselves, and the jazz musician who makes it into the filmic narrative, portrayed in a sophisticated if somewhat suspect nightclub setting, also changed how blacks were viewed. The censorship files for *Out of the Past* suggest ways in which Hollywood dealt with the issues of representation facing movie makers in 1947. As the *Out of the Past* was being made, scriptwriter Daniel Mainwaring would find himself under attack by the House Un-American Activities Committee (HUAC).[36] Abraham Polonsky, the screenwriter for *Odds Against Tomorrow*, which I discuss in chapter 8, was similarly blacklisted. RKO's management in the mid-1940s suggests that many scriptwriters and production people may have had leftist leanings and were no doubt knowledgeable about and sensitive to the cultural climate surrounding the representation of blacks in Hollywood. The script for *Out of the Past* was based on a novel by Mainwaring under his pen name, Geoffrey Homes, and James M. Cain, Mainwaring, and RKO's scriptwriter Frank Fenton all worked on it.[37] Whether or not any of these men were sensitive to the representations of blacks in Hollywood, Cain's version of the script makes no reference to blacks, sympathetic or otherwise.

An April 1946 draft with Cain's initials on it has Jeff getting information from the maid at Kathie's apartment, not a jazz club. The maid is described as "a not unappetizing cockney type," and the detective's voice-over describes her: "Oh, I caught it, don't worry, how small she was, how round, how wholly peelable, but so is a twenty-minute egg."[38] Mainwaring claims, "Cain knew he was lousy at screenwriting. . . . He hadn't the slightest idea."[39] Fenton gets most of the credit for the script, excising Cain's dubious contributions and producing a more succinct and polished version.[40] Four months later, in October, the sequence (credited to Fenton) takes place in a Harlem nightclub.

Adding a nightclub scene certainly enhances the film's timeliness. Jazz was in the news at the time. Bebop had burst onto the jazz scene with the first joint recordings of Charlie Parker and Dizzy Gillespie in New York City in 1945.[41] A jazz sequence lends the film (and the white male protagonist) an air of hipness. The PCA documents contain no references to the jazz club sequence in *Out of the Past*. Nevertheless, the sequence underwent a major and surprising revision at the script-writing phase of production. As initially scripted, on October 4, 1946, the scene is overtly racist:

CLOSEUP — trumpet as it blasts out a phrase of hot MUSIC. CAMERA PULLS BACK, revealing: Little negro joint. There is not a white man in the place until Jeff saunters in and pauses in the doorway. He looks around at the smoky walls, the shiny grinning faces of the dancers on the tiny floor, the sweating band, the row of booths crowded along the walls . . . then we see him say something to the headwaiter and the headwaiter, a gigantic dinge, leads him to the booth.[42]

Later in the sequence, Jeff seeks to bribe Eunice:

NEGRO
(to Eunice)
Maybe you better say, honey.
    EUNICE
Ah can't — much.
(as Jeff's hand moves toward the bill)
It wasn't no cold place.
(his hand retreats)
That girl, she hated snow — them clothes she took, she was lookin' for sun.
(brightening)
Florida —
    JEFF
You're sure of that?
    EUNICE
Now ah seems to remember — and ah'm sure.[43]

The script describes the jazz club as a den of black iniquity — with sweating men grinning in a smoky locale. It implies that Eunice gives Jeff the information about Kathie going to a warm place only after being offered a cash bribe. The black characters speak stereotypical Southern black slang, much like the black man in the Folgers advertisement from the 1941 *Ogden Standard Examiner* cited in chapter 2 (figure 2.12). The script calls for the characters to say *ah* instead of *I*, *mistah* instead of *mister*, *suh* instead of *sir* — a common speech pattern for Hollywood representations of blacks — although these are presumably New Yorkers. A revised script, like the one quoted above, credited to Frank Fenton, dated only a few weeks later in October, *does away* with the overtly racist portrayal, leaving a jazz sequence much like the screened version:

CLOSE SHOT—a trumpet as it blasts out a phrase of a hot number. CAMERA PANS revealing the place: there are tables, a small dance floor, a four piece orchestra. In the b.g. a headwaiter is nodding to Jeff, then leads him through the crowd toward a table in the f.g.[44]

There is no mention of race in the script; all speak standard English, no money is offered for information, and an air of sophistication reigns. The daily talent requisition for the sequence requests forty "colored" men and women, aged twenty-one to forty, "college type able and willing to dance, dark winter suits, topcoats & hats" for the men, "winter dresses or suits & hats" for the women, all "smartly dressed for niteclub."[45]

I wondered if the RKO's studio history might provide any insight into the script changes made to *Out of the Past*. The studio that produced *Citizen Kane* in 1941, as well as *King Kong* (1933), *Son of Kong* (1933) and *Mighty Joe Young* (1947), had a banner year in 1946. Betty Lasky notes that successful RKO production chief Charles Koerner died in February of 1946, and *Out of the Past*'s preproduction was almost completed before Isadore "Dore" Schary took over as head of production early in 1947.[46] Schary, "an Academy Award-winning screenwriter," who was "extremely liberal [and] a dedicated Democrat, a worshipper of the late FDR," immediately financed *Crossfire* (1947), the story of an anti-Semitic murder that was adapted from a novel in which a homosexual was the victim.[47] Although *Crossfire* was nominated for five Academy Awards in 1948, its producer, Adrian Scott, and director, Edward Dmytryk, had been charged with contempt of Congress during the HUAC hearings and fired by the studio.[48] The film received no Academy Awards. The IMDb entry indicates that *Crossfire* did win the Cannes Film Festival award for Best Social Film (1947) and the Edgar Allan Poe Award for Best Motion Picture (1948). The history of *Crossfire* suggests that liberal Hollywood insiders worked at the studio, perhaps leading to a more sympathetic representation of African Americans and others in the films produced by that studio.

Although the PCA made no specific mention of the dramatically revised jazz sequence, other matters gained the censors' attention. Two items bracket the PCA files on *Out of the Past*. The first document, a letter dated June 12, 1946, from Breen lets William Gordon at RKO Pictures know that the script is "unacceptable from the standpoint of the Production Code," primarily because the female lead lives with two different men "without being married to either of them."[49] In addition to the "gross illicit sex," the script features "an objectionably sordid flavor . . . with practically all the characters."[50] Most of the censorship and other suggestions for revision occurred at the script stage. These comments, based on an early treatment for the film by Cain, apparently damn the project. The final document, a letter (dated eight months later on Feb. 5, 1947) from RKO producer Robert Sparks to Breen's assistant, Shurlock, expresses thanks in a "note of appreciation," praising Shurlock for his "advice and derision," and "good taste in picture making."[51] I am not sure what derision means in this context, but the quote is accurate. In between these two fairly typical letters documenting the trajectory of the film through the censorship process, *Out of the Past* was produced.

Although not mentioned in the initial letter deeming the early script unacceptable, the PCA included many suggestions that "unnecessary references to liquor and drinking" be cut from the film.[52] Sex, criminality, and alcohol consumption received the censors' prohibitions. Depictions of people other than Americans were also regulated. According to the OWI, foreign audiences had to be invited into the theaters screening Hollywood movies, and the PCA helped ensure international allied cooperation during the war. The international reception of US productions and the export of an image of American culture as an ethnic melting pot were crucial to the postwar ideological project as well. The PCA helped ensure sales of films in international markets by regulating that the "just rights, history, and feelings of any nation are entitled to consideration and respectful treatment."[53]

This played a role in script revisions for *Out of the Past*. PCA records show that the Mexico sequence required specific changes to be properly respectful. Jeff, on the trail of Kathie, has followed her to Acapulco. He watches for her and sits in a sleepy cafe, La Mar Azul, with a movie theater across the street. Liam White sees the cinema outside the cafe as both a bow to the Mexican film industry and a meta-discourse on the fiction spectators watch as they watch *Out of the Past*.[54] As Jeff drowses over a drink, suddenly Kathie walks in. Jeff gets up, pulling some coins out of his pocket, and one rolls toward Kathie, seated at a table. A Mexican man, José Rodriguez (Tony Roux), walks up to them, asks Jeff to be seated, and offers them his services as a guide. They refuse him, although Jeff buys a pair of earrings. Jeff offers the jewelry to Kathie. She says she never wears them, and he responds, "Nor I." An October 17, 1946, letter from Breen to Harold Melniker at RKO makes the following suggestion:

> With regard to this Mexican sequence, please get adequate technical advice to make certain that it contains nothing offensive to the Mexicans. Specifically, on this page, the word, "spic" must be

changed. Also, please make certain that Jose is not played in an offensive manner. We also urge that he be allowed to speak grammatically correct English, with an accent, of course if you feel this is advisable for characterization.[55]

The letter cited above comes midway through the script review. In the film, José remains stereotypically oriented toward selling the Americans something when they express disinterest in having "a most excellent guide" to Acapulco. However, he speaks English with facility and leaves them to their own conversation once Jeff purchases the earrings "made of finest jade and silver."

Jeff and Kathie's love story in Acapulco develops, and Jeff waits for their evening assignations. José offers Jeff his services with a glance, and Jeff politely shakes his head, as though they meet every day, just as Jeff and Kathie meet every night. At the end of their conversation in La Mar Azul, Kathie recommends "a little cantina down the street called Pablo's." She says, "It's nice and quiet," and "a man there plays American music for a dollar; sip bourbon, shut your eyes, it's like a little place on 56th Street." Jeff proceeds to Pablo's every night, although his voice-over complains he "wasn't thinking of a joint on 56th Street." He "just thought what a sucker" he was, waiting to see Kathie again. When she does walk in, the "American music" she promised is a violin playing their theme song, "The First Time I Saw You." From Pablo's, the couple goes to another club where the man running the roulette wheel speaks French, and Kathie gambles recklessly, causing Jeff to tell her, "That isn't the way to win." She responds, "Is there a way to win?" and he suggests, "Well, there's a way to lose more slowly."

Mexico seems cosmopolitan and sophisticated, even as Jeff is drawn inexorably to Kathie and his doom, perhaps trying to "lose more slowly." By the last night of their Acapulco idyll, Kathie wears the jewelry José sold to Jeff, although she earlier claims never to wear earrings. In one of the closing sequences of the film, Jeff sees the extent of Kathie's murderous and duplicitous nature and seems fully in her grasp. Jeff says to Kathie, "We owe it all to José Rodriguez. I wonder if he'll ever know what a bad guide he was."

By facilitating Jeff's introduction to Kathie, José ensures Jeff's eventual demise. José himself is innocent, however, and no "spic" references occur. As William Luhr observes, "neither Mexico nor people of color are characterized as actively evil . . . rather both are associated with evil exclusively on a subtextual level."[56] Luhr draws the same conclusion about the Harlem

FIGURE 3.4. *In a Mexican cantina*

jazz club. I do not disagree, but I also read the sequences as offering liberation and freedom. Liam White seems to agree with me, suggesting the film "takes the idea of liberation in South America, this self-discovery south of the border to new levels."[57]

Similarly, jazz serves both the needs of the narrative and other goals as well. I never found out exactly why the rather astounding change was made to the jazz sequence in the script for *Out of the Past*. The PCA files refer directly to the representation of Mexicans but not to that of the black Americans. While the Mexico sequence undergoes almost no substantial revision, the jazz club sequence changes from overtly and stereotypically racist to stylish and respectful. Blacks, peripheral to the story, are shown living in a separate but vibrant culture. The liberal environment at RKO, the push for international and national acceptance of American products, including movies, and the overarching determination of the PCA to uphold the image of America as an ethnic melting pot produced a version of American culture in *Out of the Past*. The representation hints at the black activism implicit in bebop for an instant, suggests black life is as rich and sophisticated as white life for just a few minutes, and then the film turns its full attention back to the white narrative of sex, love, deception, murder, tax evasion, and criminality. As the PCA insists, all the criminal and questionable characters wind up dead; only the homme and femme attrapé drive off into the future. But the script revisions mitigating racism and the depiction of black lives and music as normative, however briefly, suggest that films noirs are driving America into the future, too.

CHAPTER FOUR

The Blue Gardenia, Club Pigalle, and Daniel's

CHARTING THE ALIENATION EFFECT IN FILM NOIR

*T*HE HARLEM CLUB SEQUENCE IN *OUT OF THE PAST*
(1947) portrays a particular instance of the use of jazz in
early classic film noir. The male protagonist's inevitable path to his own
doom begins there, associated with an irresistibly desirable and dangerous
woman, a trope of jazz noir. A single note intimates the dissatisfactions of
African Americans at the time, and then disappears, allowing for an instance of alienation—a thought that all might not be well with more than
just Jeff, the film's male protagonist. Here, I discuss alienation effects, or
the lack of them, in three other club sequences. First, I look at Nat King
Cole's oddly isolated performance in *The Blue Gardenia* (1953), a film that
rigorously contains black masculinity within a peculiar studio set. Then,
in *Kiss Me Deadly* (1955), in a sequence filmed in a nightclub in Los Angeles, California, the jazz club contributes emphatically to the characterization of the white male protagonist. The intimations of the single phallic
note in *Out of the Past* and the strict containment of *The Blue Gardenia* are
replaced by a more complex interaction and more pronounced alienation
effect in *Kiss Me Deadly*. Finally, in the neo-noir *Collateral* (2004), a white
hit man murders a black musician and club owner in his nightclub, eliminating the alienation effect by silencing the social and cultural ambiguity
of the jazz sequence in film noir with white male dominance over black
masculinity.

The Blue Gardenia features Cole in an oddly discrete musical sequence
where he croons the title song, a sequence that exemplifies a type of alienation effect. He and his three black band members seem to exist in a realm
entirely separate from the world of the film, although the music is nomi-

49

nally being performed by him in the nightclub that gives the film and the locale its name. Filmmakers experienced intense pressures during the two rounds of House Un-American Activities Committee (HUAC) hearings that targeted Hollywood. The first, in 1947, led to the sentencing of the "Hollywood Ten," directors and scriptwriters who refused to testify about Communist Party associations. The second was open-ended and "continued from 1951 to 1954."[1] Tom Gunning and others discuss director Fritz Lang's sense that he had been "grey-listed," not officially blacklisted by HUAC, "but not employed either."[2] For Janet Bergstrom, "deception, betrayal and psychological terrorism thoroughly penetrate this McCarthy-era film . . . a nightmare from one end to the other."[3] The nightclub sequence is no exception.

The sequence in the Blue Gardenia club accomplishes a stereotypical narrative function of jazz in film noir, despite "the Polynesian restaurant" setting and Cole singing "smooth as velvet, decked out like a cabana boy."[4] Krin Gabbard suggests that "the choice of a black jazz artist to introduce the title song is ideologically appropriate . . . in spite of the syrupy, nonjazz arrangement" of the song, as "Cole's presence [nevertheless] carried associations . . . linked . . . with loose sexuality and drug abuse."[5] Cole's song serves as a sound bridge between shots of him and shots of the protagonist, Norah (Anne Baxter), enjoying cocktails and dinner with lecherous artist Harry Prebble (Raymond Burr), but no establishing shot locates the bandstand or players within the club, and even the enthusiastically applauding audience, heard but not seen, does not share a shot with the singer. Cole's early trio included a bassist, a guitar player, and Cole on piano. The film adds a violinist to the mise-en-scène, and the soundtrack features a larger contingent of stringed instruments. Cole's playing, reflected in a strategically placed mirror above the keyboard, has almost no correspondence with the piano accompaniment. The movie did not receive great reviews, with Bosley Crowther of the *New York Times* suggesting the "happiest cast member . . . appears to be Nat (King) Cole," who "sits at a piano and sings one run-through of the title song of the picture and then goes home."[6] Bergstrom's research showed there "is virtually nothing about Nat King Cole's participation in various archives" . . . although according "to the *Los Angeles Examiner* (11 December 1952) the popular singer received $10,000 for one day's work."[7]

Only one character, an older blind woman named May (Celia Lovsky) selling blue gardenias to the club patrons, connects the singer to the restaurant. Lovsky was married to Jewish actor Peter Lorre and fled Germany with him as the Nazis came to power. She appeared in many films and television programs, and director Fritz Lang included her portrait, as

FIGURE 4.1. *Cole croons at the flower, with the mirror reflecting down on him*

gangster Lagana's beloved mother, in *The Big Heat* (1953). The blind flower seller steps incongruously into a shot of Cole at the piano and places a gardenia on the piano. Cole appears to watch her and to respond to the audience, but the sequence seems cobbled together, as though Cole never shared the studio space with the actors. A publicity still shows the actress Baxter and Cole together at the piano, but no shot of them together makes it into the film. The American Film Institute indicates the song, written and composed by Bob Russell and Lester Lee and arranged by Cole's long-time collaborator Nelson Riddle, had its debut in the film with Cole's performance.[8] As he does for "The First Time I Saw You" in *Out of the Past*, Gabbard traces the use of the song "Blue Gardenia" throughout the film in "The Vanishing Love Song in Film Noir."

The film *The Blue Gardenia* is a B-film, low-budget although made by consummate craftspeople. Bergstrom notes that "the film is based on a novel by feminist author Vera Caspary, who had also authored *Laura* and many best-selling mystery novels."[9] Caspary's "subject was the working woman, her difficulty in maintaining independence," and the film includes the home life of three young women sharing lodgings in Los Angeles.[10] Cinematographer Nicholas Musuraca shot the film, along with numerous other films noirs, including *Out of the Past*, *The Locket* (1945), and

FIGURE 4.2. *Blind flower woman (Lovsky) steps onto the bandstand*

Ida Lupino's *The Hitch-hiker* (1953). He went on to have a busy and successful career in television. Along with Baxter and Burr, Richard Conte, Ann Sothern, and other competent actors round out the cast. The narrative portrays the threat to single working-class women who share an apartment: men who all want to use them. E. Ann Kaplan writes about how the film works as a "typical film noir [in which] the world is presented from the point of view of the male" and "presents the confusion and alienation of women in a male world."[11] Prebble, the artist-letch, uses women as subjects and conquests. Conte plays Casey Mayo, a successful newspaperman. He and his photographer also take advantage of women, with a little black book and constant phone number seeking. Mayo also uses Norah for professional advancement. He publishes a "Letter to an Unknown Murderer" to lure Norah into his fame-seeking clutches, managing to entice her into his office and then pumping her for information about a crime.[12] Mayo does appear to fall in love with Norah, when he believes her to be a friend of the murderer. However, whether he falls in love with her or not does not negate Kaplan's argument. The world in this film is male and predatory; no wonder the narrative centers around a woman killing a man.

In *The Blue Gardenia*, Norah, although innocent, thinks she might have killed Prebble while fighting off his advances after a night of drinking.

The real murderer is Rose (Ruth Storey), a woman who Prebble has apparently made pregnant and refuses to marry. While Norah drunkenly swoons in the next room, Rose makes her way into Prebble's swank apartment and kills him, fittingly after he puts "their song," Richard Wagner's "Liebestod," on the turntable. Gabbard notes the complexity of the use of Wagner and "Blue Gardenia," as both tunes "slip in and out of the diegesis."[13]

Cole's physical presence, however incongruous, in *The Blue Gardenia* corresponded with his growing popularity. He whistled his way through the questions of the panelists on the well-liked television show *What's My Line* the same year (1953). According to Cole's biography his "seven chart entries were enough to rank him among the ten most successful singles artists of the year."[14] While his turn to pop music alienated some of his jazz fans, it served to increase his fame with others. Later, small-screen audiences knew the singer, as he "was [only] the fourth black performer to have his own television show."[15] Gabbard details how Cole's masculinity and sexuality were consistently held in check, noting he "was photographed from the waist up," as he is in *The Blue Gardenia*, and his early "trickster" persona receded in favor of a more sophisticated, "detached and restrained" demeanor.[16] Kaplan, perhaps because of her gender focus, misidentifies Cole as Cole Porter, a white composer and songwriter.[17] Gabbard astutely suggests "Cole was the inverse of Presley—a restrained black man acting 'white' rather than a shameless white man acting 'black.'"[18]

The Blue Gardenia uses a jazz performer as a signifier of otherness, sexuality, and danger and, at the same time, places the actual performance of the black artist above and apart from the classical performance of "Liebestod." Gabbard details how Wagner's death motif "is tied to the actual murderer" and humorously suggests the "Mickey Mousing" of the music with a "climactic act of violence," is a moment that strongly recalls a scene in Luis Buñuel's *Un chien andalou (The Andalusian Dog*, 1929).[19] The narrative seems to prefer the American pop/jazz tradition over European tradition. While it may be that German director Lang's knowledge of Wagner's Nazi sympathies helped place the opera music at the scene of the crime, the "Blue Gardenia" song is also associated with the scene of an attempted rape and a murder. With Norah's innocence proven, both tunes fade out in favor of "a grab bag of musical signifiers: the triumphant march that anchors the justice insignia . . . the fluid melody that connotes the easy camaraderie among the women . . . [and] the music of big city bustle."[20]

Cole's performance in the film seems to work for everyone, despite conflicting aims: those who already appreciated his singing—he is included in the film's marketing campaign; those film exhibitors who might want to cut a black performer from the film—his appearance is so discrete the cut might not even be noticed; those in Hollywood who wanted to show blacks involved in white life, at least as performers; and those African Americans desiring to see Cole perform in a Hollywood movie. The film represents a typically masculine noir narrative and, more subtly, the feminine version of the story. It also represents an Afro-American tale. The music sung by a black man receives top billing, while the European composer gets no credit at all. This might, in fact, be seen as Afromodernist subversion, offering a disruption to the hegemonic Hollywood system's reliance on romantic scores composed by musicians in the classical style. Cole's presence on screen also causes an alienation effect.

The strangeness of how the sequences featuring Cole are artificially inserted into the narrative causes a moment of discomfort both for the *New York Times* reviewer and for me. It marks an instance of the alienation effect in the use of jazz in film noir. In *The Blue Gardenia*, the alienation effect occurs when the narrative cannot decide how to include a black performer. Gabbard asserts that no "one associated with *Out of the Past* or *The Blue Gardenia* was objectively trying to slow the progress of African Americans toward full equality," but the filmmakers "were unable to free themselves from myths that were still present in postwar America."[21] Cole remains on screen, but the way his image is captured and contained by awkward editing and the bizarre mise-en-scène points to his disassociation from the action and causes the spectator to take note. The withheld establishing shot that would usually locate the characters with respect to one another, and Cole with respect to the patrons of the Blue Gardenia, effectively renders Cole otherworldly. He stands apart from the world of the film. To quote Brecht on the alienation effect, the musical sequence in the film "strongly resist[s] the smooth incorporation which is generally expected of it," while "lend[ing] variety to the entertainment."[22] The sequence seems to suggest blacks are thoroughly othered, yet present. Whether the oddness of the sequence reflects the intention of the filmmakers or not, the alienation effect remains the same.

Just a few years later, *Kiss Me Deadly* would also use Cole's smooth singing, containing it by having him stay safely offscreen. Nevertheless, the club sequence in this film suggests a more realistic view of black life—it was shot in an LA nightclub—and perhaps of black and white interactions. Directed by Robert Aldrich and based on a novel by hard-boiled writer Mickey Spillane, *Kiss Me Deadly* remains a perennial favorite of critics and scholars and may even be the most written about classic film noir of all, ending as it does with a nuclear explosion on a southern California beach. In my book *Dames in the Driver's Seat*, I devote a chapter titled "Apocalyptic Femmes" to the film.[23] The less than brilliant male protagonist, Mike Hammer (Ralph Meeker), abuses his enemies, his friends, and his lover, but the jazz sequence, filmed in Club Pigalle on Figueroa Street, presents a different Hammer.

Like the Porters and Waiters Club in Ogden, Club Pigalle served African American patrons. According to Meredith Drake Reitan, the club was owned by boxing champion Willy Bean and managed by boxer Chalky Wright, whose name resonates with Chalky White, a character in the television series *Boardwalk Empire*.[24] In October 1954, *Jet* mentions Club Pigalle as the locale for a chitterling-eating contest between singers Lawrence Stone and Ernie Andrews, and it mentions the club again in 1958 as the owner, now Leroy Baskerville, "faces claims from employees and social clubs who say he pocketed advances for club dates."[25] Like the Porters and Waiters Club, Club Pigalle existed separate from Hollywood.

As James Naremore comments, the Club Pigalle sequence makes the otherwise despicable Mike Hammer momentarily into "a relatively sympathetic embodiment of urban liberalism."[26] Naremore continues, "when we first meet Hammer he is listening to Nat Cole on the radio; later we discover that he is a regular customer at an all-black jazz club, where his friendship with a black singer (Madi Comfort) and a black bartender (Art Loggins) helps to indicate his essential hipness."[27] This is true, but there is more than hipness at stake in this scene. The bartender and singer are comfortably familiar with the white male protagonist as well. They seem to know a different Hammer than the one otherwise portrayed on the screen. They appear to genuinely like him and sympathize with his sorrow and fear. Hammer's affectionate relationship with these black characters seems remarkable, especially in the face of his overt misogyny and even misanthropy toward other characters. The audience needs to see these minor players' feelings for Hammer in order to gain a richer understanding of his character.

But who are Madi Comfort and Art Loggins, the bit actors in the most famous film noir? Art Loggins appears in no other films and is not listed in any biographical records. A comprehensive search of reference sources on jazz, music, musicals, blacks in film, black Americans, film, and film noir yields no information beyond the fact that both actors appeared in *Kiss Me Deadly*. A 2003 online obituary for Madi Comfort asserts that she performed with Ellington's band in the early 1950s, that Ellington wrote the 1956 hit song "Satin Doll" for her, and that she and Ellington appear in *Kiss Me Deadly*.[28] I do not see Ellington on screen. Comfort donated a picture to *Shades of California: The Hidden Beauty of Ordinary Life* that shows her dancing with her new husband, bassist Joseph Comfort, "to Jimmy Lunceford's band at the Plantation Club."[29] The picture caption goes on to say Joe Comfort "played with Nat King Cole, Lionel Hampton, Ella Fitzgerald and Duke Ellington," reiterating that "Madi was the 'Satin Doll' of Duke Ellington's song."[30] Director Aldrich mentions that he had more trouble from the censors with how she held the microphone than he did any other aspects of the film.[31] This is interesting enough for a story, but it reveals nothing further about who Madi Comfort was. More promising are the later online reports connecting Comfort to the unsolved Black Dahlia case, suggesting she associated with a primary suspect in that murder. But even if that lent authenticity to her as a casting choice, the audience could not have known that. Fortunately, both she and Loggins play their film roles effectively.

The jazz club sequence opens with Comfort in a sexy, light-colored dress holding a microphone and singing the same song Cole sings earlier. Comfort mimes "I'd Rather Have the Blues Than What I've Got" with piano accompaniment. Tony Williams elaborates, saying Comfort performs the tune "in the manner of a cabaret torch singer, [and] the lines 'The web has got me caught' and 'I'd rather have the blues than what I've got' evocatively compliment the film's narrative."[32] Sitting at the bar, Hammer, whose friend and car mechanic Nick has just been murdered, listens to the performance appreciatively, if sadly. As with Jeff in the Harlem jazz club, Hammer appears to be the only white guy in the place, a sophisticated club full of patrons drinking, smoking, and listening attentively. But unlike Jeff's, Hammer's presence there seems habitual; the bartender expresses concern for him, and Hammer buys him a drink. A dissolve indicates the passage of time; only the singer, bartender, and Hammer, now passed out on the bar, remain. Another white man talks to the barkeep and leaves. Hammer's girlfriend, Velda, has been kidnapped. He gets up and stumbles toward the door. The singer says, "I'm sorry, Mike," and he responds, "Thanks, kid." David Butler notes that in "the original script, the [attractive] singer appear[s] keen to meet with Hammer . . . and he touches her cheek as he leaves the bar."[33] (46). Although this potential "romantic or sexual encounter between Hammer and the black singer" is left out of the film, the tenderness remains.[34]

In fact, jazz singer Kitty White actually sings "I'd Rather Have the Blues" in the film, while Comfort lip-synchs. White is listed in various sources as the uncredited vocalist in the club, and her name shows up in the opening credits, along with Cole's. Cole sings the same song as Comfort/White in the opening sequence of the film, although not on screen, his voice emanating diegetically from Hammer's car radio. In that

FIGURE 4.3. *Hammer and the sympathetic bartender*

FIGURE 4.4. *Jazz chanteuse*

sequence, Hammer has just picked up a desperate woman (Cloris Leachman) who runs down the road clad only in a raincoat. Her frightened breathing and gasping sounds louder than Cole's singing, disturbing the crooner's rendition of the song. The threat implied by jazz again makes itself manifest. The spectator does not know what makes the woman so fearful, but the jazz provides the soundtrack and recedes in the face of her

FIGURE 4.5. *"They got your girl."*

terror. Gabbard suggests Cole's success as a film and television presence were in part due to his restraint; his "sexuality and racial difference are both acknowledged and denied in most films, his otherness . . . excessively contained."[35] *Kiss Me Deadly* presents jazz as hip and black, but restrained and accessible through the crooning of Cole while he remains invisible.

Jazz, therefore, whether performed on screen or diegetically heard on the radio, informs this famous film noir. The narrative flow and the cohesive characterization of Hammer as a jerk are disrupted by his brief foray into black culture. The alienation effect lasts just a bit longer than in *Out of the Past* and seems less incidental than in *The Blue Gardenia*. By 1955, black militancy—musical and social—was impossible to ignore. Rosa Parks refused to give up her bus seat to a white man in 1955, the same year *Kiss Me Deadly* first appeared in theaters.[36] Racial tension does not emerge in the narrative of the film but certainly circulated in the atmosphere at the time of its release. *Out of the Past* does not dwell on (or in) the jazz club, although it represents the culture vibrantly. In contrast, by the mid-1950s Hollywood acknowledges black jazz as firmly rooted in the urban (California) landscape and implies some white sympathy and perhaps even involvement in the black struggle for social equality.[37]

Neo-noir, which draws on classic noir style and narratives but is made and set in the present, uses jazz differently. In the twenty-first century, Hollywood neo-noirs still venture into the jazz clubs, but the struggle for social equality hinted at by *Out of the Past*, *The Blue Gardenia*, and *Kiss Me Deadly* becomes less visible, at least in *Collateral*. *Collateral* (Mann 2004) provides a slick derivation of the classic film noir *This Gun for Hire* (Tuttle 1942), with Tom Cruise playing the efficient hit man apparently brutalized by an abusive childhood (Alan Ladd's role in the classic film noir) and Jamie Foxx (in the Veronica Lake role) playing the role of a law-abiding citizen coerced into assisting a contract killer carry out his murders. The hit man's assistant has become a black man instead of a white woman, but much of the dynamic between the two character remains as it was in the classic noir—with the exception that sexual sparks do not seem to ignite when Cruise and Foxx share the screen—and Vincent (Cruise's character) offers Max (Foxx's character) suggestions on how to achieve the American Dream. The white man teaches the black man how to succeed.

About a third of the way into *Collateral*, hit man Vincent and LA taxi driver Max stop at a jazz club called Daniel's on Leimart Boulevard, a place where, according to Vincent, all the West Coast jazz greats—Dexter Gordon, Charles Mingus, Chet Baker—once played. The club does not actually exist, although the exteriors were filmed in Los Angeles near a bar called Cheerios. In the club, Vincent listens to the black jazz band and lead trumpet player Daniel (Barry "Shabaka" Henley) play, while he pontificates to the less knowledgeable Max about improvising and playing behind the notes. Gabbard tells me Henley is pantomiming, playing music from Miles Davis's *Bitches Brew* album, a strange choice since the jazz nerds at the movies would surely recognize it as not improvisation.[38] Davis appears in the diegetic soundtrack, for those who know jazz. The jazz session ends as the camera pans over to a partially obscured poster of John Coltrane, famed saxophone player and Davis's sometime collaborator. The sequence concludes with the hit man inviting Daniel over to his table, buying him a drink and then shooting him.[39]

Well, not that abruptly. First, Vincent talks with Daniel about the phenomenal skill of Davis, one of the great innovators of late bebop, among many other important jazz idioms. I will explore Davis's contribution to classic noir in the French film *Ascenseur Pour L'Echafaud* (Elevator to the Gallows) in chapter 6. For now, it is important to note only that in *Collateral* the racial aspects of Davis's militancy are ignored in favor of an appeal to phallic artistry. Daniel mentions Davis was "the coolest man on the planet" and "a scary cat" but does not connect his intensity with anything but his devotion to the music. Daniel does admit he was born the day he played with Davis. Gary Giddins and Scott DeVeaux describe Davis as "the archetypal modern jazz musician (distant, unflappable, romantic) and the civil-rights era black man (self-reliant, outspoken, confident)."[40] However, despite his assertive black masculinity and self-reliance, for Davis it was always about the music. As DeVeaux notes, Davis's "1949–1950 *Birth*

FIGURE 4.6. *Jazz club in Los Angeles*

of the Cool band" served as a "vibrant symbol" of "racial cooperation."[41] So
the next seconds of the narrative are jarring anyway, but especially so to
anyone familiar with jazz generally and the life and music of Miles Davis
specifically. Immediately after this conversation, the white male protagonist reasserts his own white phallic dominance by shooting Daniel after
agreeing to let the horn-player live if he can correctly answer a question
about Davis. Of course, the jazz question Vincent asks Daniel is just a ruse;
he never planned to do anything but his job, displaying the same Protes-
tant work ethic and rugged individualism the black taxi driver and the jazz
musician supposedly lack. *Collateral* revises a jazz sequence that once implied black militancy and white responses to racial inequality in favor of
total white control, tamping down any possible alienation effect.

Jazz and film noir are intimately linked, with classic film noir in the
1940s and 1950s obliquely providing a historiography of jazz through the
lens of the movie camera, a Hollywood-style map of musical, racial, and
cultural tensions in black and white. Neo-noirs often revise gender roles
while providing reactionary representations of race. *Collateral* recognizes
the film noir/jazz connection but uses the nightclub sequence unambigu-
ously to confirm white male power over black militancy. Despite that con-
firmation, the black taxi driver survives the narrative, albeit as a *homme
attrapé* willing to work within society's rules, while the white criminal
does not. This reaffirms the outdated morality of classic films noirs upheld
for years by the Production Code Administration, even as it defuses the
possibility of black expressions of power through jazz.

CHAPTER FIVE

From Elysian to Robards, from Real to Reel

*T*HE JAZZ CLUBS IN *SWEET SMELL OF SUCCESS* (1957) take a young lover from the Elysian Club and a promise of paradise to Robards and a state of despair. While the cold, glistening nighttime Manhattan cityscapes are real, both the clubs, as well as all the interiors in the film, were created and shot in a Hollywood studio. The film features a classical Hollywood score composed by Elmer Bernstein and music composed and performed by the mixed-race Chico Hamilton Quintet. The jazz musicians appear on screen and add definitively to the characterization of a white Hollywood actor playing the leader of a jazz quintet. The combination of the sound and appearance of the real within the fabricated world of classic film noir creates a unique alienation effect, but the final and overwhelming notes remain in the dominant discourse of Hollywood.

Sweet Smell of Success features young lovers, marvelously smart and bitter dialogue, an unrelentingly bleak view of its protagonists — not the lovers but a gossip columnist and a press agent — and a glimpse into a sophisticated jazz scene that serves as an unusual, although ultimately unsuccessful, artistic antidote to that bleakness. Before seeing the movie, I had read that West Coast jazz drummer Chico Hamilton and his quintet, including composer and cellist Fred Katz, appear on screen, playing music and with speaking parts. In his essay on the music in the film, David Butler mentions the Hamilton Quintet's "'chamber jazz' sensibility [which] blurs the traditional distinction that Hollywood made between black jazz, usually portrayed as hot, rhythmic, and impulsive, and white classical music, often encoded as serious, intellectual, and thus culturally superior."[1] The group embodies Afromodernism, using "discursive strategies from outside the African-American cultural set . . . [in] the act of advancing African-American presence."[2] However, their potentially radical presence in the film is contained by Elmer Bernstein's occasionally jazzy and often melodramatic Hollywood score. As Butler notes, Bernstein's score reinforces jazz stereotypes, with "big band textures and bluesy into-nation for the night-time shots of the city with its sleaze and corruption, whereas the white couple's romance is played out to the accompaniment of large-scale, legato string orchestration."[3] Nevertheless, the sound of Hamilton's jazz and the musicians' hip and sophisticated presence help characterize the otherwise completely bland white hero. For the all-to-brief minutes when jazz and jazz musicians take center screen, the alienation effect comes into focus. Jazz functions as the soundtrack but also functions as jazz, completely separated from the storyline. The narrative concerns white men and their power plays. Yet a black man figures distinctly in the background, and jazz music, composed and played by black and white musicians on screen, invests the film with elements beyond those overtly taken up by the narrative. The change in the representation of jazz in Hollywood in the ten years that separate *Out of the Past* from *Sweet Smell of Success* represents both how far US cultural and race relations had come and how little had changed.

But before considering the two jazz sequences, I will examine the production history of the film, featuring notorious egos, actors turned producers, the inescapable impact of the House Un-American Activities Committee (HUAC), and the "ripped from the headlines" inspiration for the tale. The story turns on the love of Susan (Susan Harrison) for a young leader of a jazz quintet, Steve (Martin Milner), and on press agent Sidney's (Tony Curtis) desperate drive to align himself with the powerful, ruthless, and hugely popular gossip columnist, J. J. Hunsecker (Burt Lancaster), Susan's possessive brother. Sidney, Hunsecker, and the corrupt and sweaty police sergeant Harry Kello (Emile Meyer) engage in fast-paced, brutal, and often funny repartee. James Naremore describes scriptwriter Clifford Odets as a well-known leftist playwright in the 1930s who had fallen from popular favor in Hollywood for naming names during the HUAC hearings.[4] Odets was a friendly witness in 1952 but only named those who had already been identified by other witnesses. Odets gets most of the credit for the lively verbal acuity of the main characters. These audacious, heartless schemers easily outshine and outtalk the low-key and bland young lovers whose relationship provides the source of the trouble in the narrative. The young man, Steve, although the lead guitarist in a jazz quintet, lacks any artistic passion and arouses only Susan.

Susan's ostentatious fur coat should signal her femme fatale status to the spectator, but she does not drive the narrative until the final sequences and even then manages her corrective duplicity primarily through passivity rather than action. Hunsecker enlists his conflicted but willing sycophant, Sidney, to break up the lovers. Sidney works first through subterfuge, planting a story that Steve is a communist and drug user. Finally, fully aware of the despicable nature of his actions yet desperate to win Hunsecker's approval, Sidney plants marijuana cigarettes in Steve's coat pocket while he plays a gig at a club called Robards. Sidney tips off Kello, the unethical sergeant, leading to a brutal beating that leaves Steve hospitalized. Susan, much more a femme attrapée, or woman trapped by the patriarchy, than a femme fatale throughout the movie, finally also turns duplicitous. Her brother enters the luxurious penthouse apartment he shares with Susan to find Sidney there and Susan half-undressed and distressed. He infers that Sidney attacked her. Instead Sidney had just prevented her from throwing herself off the balcony in despair, but Susan, passive and yet fully aware, remains silent as her brother draws his conclusions and metes out his revenge. The sadistic Kello will catch up with Sidney on the street. The film ends as Susan leaves the apartment on her way to her lover.

Sweet Smell originated as a novella by Ernest Lehman, who had worked for a Broadway publicist named Irving Hoffman and who drew inspiration from Hoffman's relationship with powerful gossip columnist Walter Winchell.[5] Supporting Franklin D. Roosevelt and opposing Hitler early in his career, "in the postwar era he [Winchell] morphed into a rabid anti-communist and vicious rumor monger" who associated with Joseph McCarthy.[6] In addition, Winchell "was obsessively and some believed unnaturally attached to his daughter, Walda" even giving "her a fabulous mink coat" for "her eighteenth birthday."[7] Lehman, originally hired to direct the film, relinquished the task for health reasons.[8] With Lehman out as director, producers choose American-born but Scotland-raised Alexander Mackendrick, whose career up until *Sweet Smell* had been with Britain's Ealing Studios.[9] Mackendrick lobbied to have Odets, "one of his cultural heroes," to assist with the screenplay.[10] Odets' career was languishing, and he was seen to be a traitor by other leftists when he started work on *Sweet Smell*.[11]

Director Mackendrick details the process of working with Odets, saying he "dismantled the structure of every single sequence in order to rebuild situations and relationships . . . that were more complex and had much greater tension and anxiety."[12] The dialogue of the film snaps and sizzles, providing Hunsecker with lines such as "Match me, Sidney," and "I wouldn't want to take a bite out of you. You're a cookie full of arsenic." Sidney also fulfills the hard-boiled necessity for verbal acuity in film noir. When he manages to set up the innocent jazzman for a bust, he tells Hunsecker, "The cat's in the bag and the bag's in the river." The crooked cop Kello gets some of the most overtly threatening lines, made more malevolent by his thickly accented and humorous delivery. He threatens Sidney, saying, "Come back, Sidney, I wanna chastise you." Mackendrick makes it clear that the energy of the characterizations comes from Odets.[13]

Although Winchell, who inspired the character of Hunsecker, was a small man, the producers, including Lancaster, considered Orson Welles for the role until Lancaster decided he wanted the part.[14] A former circus performer and physically imposing, the liberal Lancaster got his Hollywood start in the quintessential film noir *The Killers* and had just finished playing Wyatt Earp in *Gunfight at the OK Corral* (1957) and starring in *The Rainmaker* (1956) with Katharine Hepburn. He and Tony Curtis, his costar and coproducer of *Sweet Smell*, had recently increased their popularity playing men in tights in *Trapeze* (1956). Like many successful Hollywood actors and performers, including Ida Lupino and Harry Belafonte, Lancaster started his own production company in the late 1940s; by 1957 the company included Lancaster, agent Harold Hecht, and "James Hill, a former writer at MGM, who worked as a producer on *Trapeze*."[15] They called themselves Hecht-Hill-Lancaster (HHL), and *Sweet Smell* became one of the first movies the three produced. It also proved their least successful, although time has increased its popularity.

The Production Code Administration (PCA) and Breen initially rejected the short story that inspired the film. Breen's May 19, 1949, letter objects to the following elements:

> First, the suggestion of an incestuous love between the columnist, Hunsecker, and his sister, Susan.
>
> Second, the use of marijuana cigarettes planted on an innocent party to obtain his arrest.
>
> Third, the final scene in which the girl strips herself, accuses the lead of attempted rape, and (apparently) brings about his murder at the hands of her enraged brother—which constitutes murder without any indicated punishment.[16]

Despite these objections, the suggestion of an incestuous love and the use of marijuana cigarettes both remain in the film, albeit downplayed. In the final sequence, Susan's accusation occurs more subtly and passively, and Kello metes out the final punishment for Sidney. Subsequent suggestions detailed in a letter from Geoffrey Shurlock to producer Hecht focus more on sex, especially regarding Rita (Barbara Nichols), a female friend who Sidney sets up with a lecherous man to further his goals.[17] While some of the dialogue is eased, the implications of Sidney's selling of Rita's body remain the same. No wonder some spectators did not like the film.

Still, many critics do like it. For example, David Denby, of *New York* magazine and the *New Yorker*, counts *Sweet Smell* as one of the most quintessential New York movies, saying, "This downbeat, black-and-white production . . . starring Burt Lancaster as a blackmailing newspaper columnist and Tony Curtis as a hustling press agent, has a special wised-up, acrid flavor that seems the essence of New York cynicism."[18] And it is no wonder. The city plays a crucial role in the film from beginning to end. James Wong Howe, who developed deep focus photography before Gregg Toland made it famous in *Citizen Kane*, contributes his skills to the brilliant, often rain-soaked and shiny cinematography. *Sweet Smell* opens with Academy Award–winning cinematographer Howe's "montage of Manhattan streets at night," "deliberately evocative of the 'New York School' of street photographers in the 1940s and 1950s, and [marking] the film from the beginning with an iconic noir-ness."[19] As Mark Feeney notes, the film brings to mind New York photographer Weegee and the lonely urban photographic landscapes of Alfred Stieglitz.[20] Bernstein's "shrill, jazzy main-title theme" accompanies the energetic opening sequence.[21] It is, as Denby says, the essence of New York, and it is that way by design.

As Director Mackendrick explains, "I liked the idea of trying to capture on screen the atmosphere of Manhattan . . . particularly the square mile that constitutes the area between Forty-second Street and Fifty-seventh Street (the theater and nightclub district) . . . [and] the neurotic energy of the crowded sidewalks."[22] On a trip to New York to scout locations, Howe, Mackendrick, and art director Edward Carrere "developed the formula of starting many of the scenes in exteriors, beginning with short passages of dialogue on the claustrophobic Manhattan streets outside . . . before following the character into the interiors."[23] The film manages to seamlessly connect the location shooting of the New York street sequences with the California studio-created interiors using this device. Aiding in that seamless connection is jazz. As I will show, it serves as a bridge.

Bernstein's nondiegetic jazz-inflected score dominates most of the film, and the shots of the nighttime streets glisten with oily wetness and energy. For the club interiors, Rob Nixon writes that Howe "had the walls and ceilings smeared with oil to give the sets a slimy sheen and carry the look of the dirty, rain soaked streets indoors," and even "fit Lancaster with thick glasses, often smudged with oil, that when lit closely from a high angle, would deepen his eye sockets and produce . . . a mask like effect."[24] This "slimy sheen" certainly suits the main characters, Sidney and Hunsecker, and the Bernstein score elaborates on that sheen.

FIGURE 5.1. *The eyes of Hunsecker*

Bernstein's jazzy big-band sound opens the film, providing audio re-inforcement in the film's first minutes. The street shots of that initial sequence also provide the first image of J. J. Hunsecker as a newspaper delivery truck leaves a busy warehouse and makes its way through crowded streets "bearing a sign: 'Go with The Globe: Read J. J. Hunsecker, The Eyes of Broadway,'" with "Hunsecker's eyes and eyeglasses" above the sign.[25]

Even after the character of Hunsecker has made his physical appearance on screen, in many later sequences, the posters, flyers, and headlines ensure that he is always watching even if not physically present. Gary Giddins uses the eyes to make an astute connection to another tale of "lies and corruption," *The Great Gatsby*'s ash heap billboard of the eyes of Doctor T. J. Eckleburg."[26] Dr. Eckleburg also watches over a wasteland of corruption as Nick, the narrator of *The Great Gatsby*, sees it. The novel uses the optometrist's advertisement to mark the decadence of the Jazz Age and the existential emptiness of it all; Hunsecker's eyes mark the inescapable extent of his power. Hunsecker, like Gatsby, does not appear until midway through the film, although his power and influence drive the narrative from the opening scenes. Giddins suggests this "exemplifies what Orson Welles . . . described as a Mr. Wu device . . . for an hour, everyone talks about the mysterious Mr. Wu, so that his arrival is the . . . dramatic high point."[27] When Hunsecker does appear, he treats everyone with sneering brutality—all four people at his table at the 21 Club, including a senator and his young paramour.[28] For me, however, the high points are the sequences that take place in jazz clubs, not in the 21 Club, despite the brilliant, caustic dialogue. In the two brief sequences that feature musicians in a club setting, the jazz actually follows the characters back outside to the street.

The first club sequence takes place at the Elysian and introduces the group Steve leads, actually the Chico Hamilton Quintet. The West Coast band included an unusual combination of musicians for a small jazz group: drummer Hamilton, "Buddy Collette on reeds, . . . guitarist Jim Hall, bassist Carson Smith and . . . the cellist Fred Katz."[29] In an interview with Mark Myers from March of 2003, Hamilton recalls working with amazing musicians even in high school, where the jazz band included Dexter Gordon, Charles Mingus, Buddy Collette, and Illinois Jacquet, among other future jazz greats. The talented young drummer played with Gerry Mulligan, backed Lena Horne in Europe and the US, worked with Billie Holiday, and even discovered Eric Dolphy.[30] Hamilton talks about his original 1955 quintet playing in a "funky" club in Long Beach, saying, "Can you imagine? Two black dudes and three white dudes going into a place like that with a cello. I tell you, man . . . half the time we had to fight our way out of there. But the whole world dug our sound."[31] Here, Hamilton seems well aware of the subversion his group manifests, and even states his willingness to fight for it.

Hamilton's foray into Hollywood music did not happen without some careful detective work by the film's producers. Drugs and jazz were intimately connected in the public consciousness with, for example, drummer Gene Krupa's arrest involving marijuana cigarettes in 1943, Billie Holiday's constant battle with drugs in the late 1940s and 1950s, the death of Charlie Parker in 1955, and Gerry Mulligan's 1954 drug bust. Drugs also feature in the film narrative, making the filmmakers especially vigilant with the players. Hamilton notes that the filmmakers insisted he and his fellow musicians be assiduously drug free, even following them for "six months . . . to make sure there was no dope in my band. . . . They definitely wanted to make sure we were clean."[32] The sound of Hamilton's quintet, cool, cerebral, "chamber jazz . . . blend[ing] aspects of classical music with jazz," shows up modestly in *Sweet Smell*, allowing West Coast jazz to seep out of the clubs and onto the streets of New York City.[33]

The first club sequence begins with the quintet in the foreground as Steve counts down to the beginning of a number, called "Sidney's Theme" on the Cherry Red Records soundtrack album, which includes the compositions from the Chico Hamilton Quintet and Elmer Bernstein.[34] The camera focuses on the bassist, then Hamilton on the cymbals, then the flute player, Paul Horn, who replaced Buddy Collette, then Fred Katz on cello, and finally Steve. Katz's curly dark hair and horn-rimmed glasses make him look more like a young college professor than a jazz musician.[35] By 1956, in addition to Katz, who receives composing credit with Hamilton, the quintet included John Pisano, who replaced Jim Hall on guitar.

Sources debate whether Hall or Pisano serves as the source of Steve's playing in the film; Krin Gabbard, David Meeker, and Yannow all mention Hall.[36] Hamilton, however, verifies that Pisano worked on the film. According to Hamilton, "The actor Martin Milner [Steve] ... didn't know how to play guitar ... [so] Milner put his left hand behind him and John Pisano, my guitar player, put his hand on the strings. ... It looked like Milner was playing the guitar, the way Jimmy Wong [Howe] shot it."[37] For Morris Holbrook, the distinction between guitarists Pisano and Hall was crucial to understanding Steve, since the character "[is] ... rather *bland*" and so is the "competent but essentially routine journey-man guitar" playing of Pisano; this helps create a "character lacking in uniqueness or individuality."[38] Holbrook contrasts Hall's guitar playing, filled with "engaged involvement, stubborn uniqueness, and singular individuality" as well as "understated complexity" with the dullness of Pisano's playing.[39]

No doubt guitarists could play a certain way as well as actors act, especially in the limited confines of incidental music for a film. Yet the attention to Steve's characterization makes sense. Milner had already played a jazz musician, the drunken drummer in *Pete Kelly's Blues* (1955).[40] In *Sweet Smell*, most spectators see Steve as perhaps bland, but also, as Gabbard suggests, a man who "cannot be bought or corrupted ... the film's one exemplary character."[41] Giddins sees Steve as "more like Hunsecker. ... They are both prigs, self-righteous and combative," and I agree.[42] Giddins elaborates, writing that "Susie is accustomed to being smothered, and Steve is willing to take over that task from her brother."[43] Steve provides Susan with an alternative to her incestuously tinged relationship with her brother, but she remains powerless against both men. Denise Mann uses Michel Foucault to interpret the film, calling Hunsecker's gaze "disciplinary" and Susan the "docile body" who is oppressed by those around her.[44] Perhaps Steve's priggishness does reflect in Pisano's uninspired guitar playing, just as Hunsecker's oppressive rigidity reflects in Lancaster's upright and still body. The more important takeaway, however, is the discussion about the music. The music is the bridge.

The sequence introducing Steve also allows Hamilton and his band members their brief foray into acting in a Hollywood movie. After their set, an avid female jazz fan in horn-rimmed glasses, identified by the script as "Intellectual Young Woman," corners Steve, suggesting the jazz they play is "an interesting fusion of the traditional, classical form and the new progressive style," providing an accurate description of the quintet's music.[45] Meanwhile, Hamilton sees Susan waiting for Steve in the alley behind the club and tells Paul Horn to "cool this chick here while I go get Steve," a line Hamilton says he suggested to Mackendrick.[46] Here, just as New York City serves as an authentic setting for the film, Hamilton, a real West Coast jazz musician, serves as an authentic filmed version of himself. In *Anatomy of a Murder*, Duke Ellington appears on screen as Pie Eye, a jazz bandleader in a club on Michigan's Upper Peninsula. Although *Anatomy* uses location shooting for the interiors and exteriors, the drive for realism does not extend to having Duke Ellington play himself. Here, Hamilton acts as himself—he and his band members provide a hip sheen to Steve's characterization, despite Pisano's guitar playing.

Steve manages to extricate himself from the "much-too-earnest devotee of progressive jazz" by turning her attention to the surprised Katz, who Steve says "writes the stuff," and goes out to Susie, as he calls her, in the alley behind the club.[47] As Horn reenters the club and closes the door, leaving Steve and Susan alone, intermission piano music played between the quintet's sets begins and accompanies the early part of the scene as Susan tells Steve she will marry him. The script identifies the "intermission pianist" as Jerry Wiggins.[48] The piano soundtrack also has the muted sounds of a crowded club and car traffic in the background, yet it now seems nondiegetic, as the volume does not vary with the opening and closing of the stage door. Minutes later, backstage, Sidney looks for Steve, asking the quintet about his location. Hamilton deliberately misleads him, saying "unhelpfully," that Steve is "upstairs, maybe."[49] Meanwhile, out in the alley, Bernstein's more symphonic and melodramatic nondiegetic scoring takes over, with strings dominating as Steve tells Susan he wants to dedicate the next number and all the rest to her and suggests they go out and celebrate the good news with the boys, meaning his band. She demurs since she has not yet told her brother about Steve. Just then, Sidney interrupts the lovers, and the piano jazz comes out into the alleyway with him.

During the showdown between Steve and Sidney out behind the club, Hamilton remains visible in the background, looking on with engaged interest, as though he is ready to defend Steve. Hamilton, with his fine posture and groovy, well-fitted suit, supports Steve's affair with Susan both verbally and by his strong presence. The other members of the quintet, without speaking roles, also look on with studied interest. In *Out of the Past*, the detective goes to a Harlem jazz club to gather information about the femme fatale from her black maid. Neither character gives or gets much information, but their actions add a patina of liberal white hipness. A similar but more emphatic liberal white hipness attaches itself

FIGURE 5.2. *The bandmates stand ready*

to Steve, whose interactions with his bandmates indicate respect and equality between the men, regardless of race. Gabbard elaborates, saying the Steve operates "at the nexus of thoughtful music and borrowed black manliness."[50]

Sidney and Steve start a verbal spat that eventually brings Steve's agent Frank D'Angelo, who is also Sidney's uncle, and the band onto the metal stairs behind the building. Sam Levine (who plays homme attrapé to Lancaster's homme fatal in *The Killers* and the Jewish man murdered early in *Crossfire*) plays D'Angelo. As the camera reenters the club, Wiggins, the pianist, finishes playing a tune, marking a sophisticated complication in the diegetic/nondiegetic distinction. Richard Ness sees this "breakdown of traditional diegetic/nondiegetic distinctions" as a "destabilizing device" typical of the "music for *noir* films."[51]

The same breakdown happens again as Steve and his quintet start playing again onstage inside the club, now a lyrical, almost classical theme called "Susan: The Sage" on the soundtrack. The guitar-oriented composition follows Sidney and Susan out onto the street. As they wait for a taxi in front of a billboard advertising the quintet, they converse to the accompaniment of the guitar. Again, when the club door closes, the volume remains stable, so what started as diegetic music, with a source on screen, becomes subtly nondiegetic. When Susie and Sidney's cab door closes on them, the apparently nondiegetic music stops, and they converse without musical accompaniment. For me, the connection of the jazz with Sidney humanizes a character that seems otherwise despicable, just as it does for

Hammer in *Kiss me Deadly*. Sophisticated and classical-infused jazz, associated with Chico and his bandmates who are represented as serious artists, bolsters Steve's characterization and even provides Sidney's oily sheen with just a smidgen of humanity. Sidney's association with nondiegetic jazz scoring and Curtis's remarkable acting hint at decency, or at least conscience, even as Sidney continues to ruin everything and everyone to please Hunsecker.

Just as writers differ on the guitarists playing on the soundtrack, they also "confuse Elmer Bernstein's nondiegetic score with the music played by Chico Hamilton's quintet."[52] Apparently, Katz and Hamilton "had provided an entire score, but . . . it was almost entirely discarded when the studio brought Bernstein into the project."[53] So, for a moment in its production history, *Sweet Smell* threatened to be the first Hollywood film to feature a score composed by working jazz musicians, a threat made good by Ellington and Strayhorn with *Anatomy* just two years later. With the addition of Bernstein, the score changed from potentially revolutionary to typical, although jazz flavored, Hollywood practice. Giddins suggests that Bernstein's "massed brasses and shuffle rhythms . . . contrasted agreeably with Hamilton's lightly astringent approach," and that Bernstein "balanced the jazz cues with more traditional ones."[54] In *Sweet Smell*, a conflicted view of jazz emerges, with Hamilton's chamber jazz contrasting with Bernstein's jazz-inflected score. Just as the Chico Hamilton Quintet's fusion of jazz and classical idioms along with white and black musicians

FIGURE 5.3. *A conversation on the street*

distanced jazz from typical associations with drug use and tortured genius, the music played by the quintet in *Sweet Smell* alienates jazz from the common Hollywood associations of sleaze and otherness, suggesting instead sophisticated artistry.

The soundtrack album identifies eight songs by the Chico Hamilton Quintet, along with four others composed by Hamilton and Katz but conducted by Elmer Bernstein with orchestration by Leo Shuken and Jack Hayes. Bernstein has credit for writing ten additional tunes. Bernstein had composed for film just a few years earlier for *The Man with the Golden Arm* with the assistance of jazzmen Shorty Rogers and Shelly Manne, but, he insisted his "jazz scores have never been pure jazz but jazz-inflected."[55] Bernstein came to regret the success of the score for *The Man with the Golden Arm*, saying, "Now there are a rash of unpleasant films using jazz more or less skillfully."[56] Butler clarifies the scoring for *Sweet Smell*, writing that the "Chico Hamilton quintet did not play the entire score, but neither did Elmer Bernstein compose the music performed by the quintet. The Hamilton group is heard only in those sequences where they play diegetically. The nondiegetic score, however, was composed by Bernstein and performed by a studio orchestra."[57] As I have shown, this is not entirely accurate, since Hamilton and Katz's music leaks over into the street and the action of the film separate from the jazz club. This spilling over provides a sound bridge to the location shooting on the Manhattan streets, making a graceful and implicit connection between the studio sets and location shots. It also serves, subtly, to keep the spectator's sympathy with Sidney, even as he commits egregious acts.

The second and last jazz club sequence takes place in another studio-created club called Robards. Steve and the quintet play a tune called "Goodbye Baby" as Sidney talks with D'Angelo, who assures Sidney that Steve and Susie have called it quits. Sidney overhears the manager telling the club owner that Steve is not feeling well and needs to leave early. Sidney surreptitiously plants the pack of marijuana-laced cigarettes in Steve's overcoat pocket and leaves the club. Once again the jazz, now what seems to be a version of "Susan: The Sage," follows him out onto the street, becoming nondiegetic as Sidney interacts with Kello who, thanks to Sidney, waits to arrest Steve outside the club. Sidney responds to the taunting of the cop with taunts of his own, calling Kello "sweaty" as he climbs stairs up to a higher street level. Once there, he looks down on the club entrance and the police car in the night. The camera reenters the club, and as Steve steps down off the stage, jazz trombonist Frank Rosolino and his combo, including trumpet player Conte Candoli and a bass man, join Hamilton onstage and start playing.

FIGURE 5.4. *Hamilton's explosive drum solo*

The lively tune, called "Jam" on the soundtrack album, now accompanies Steve out onto the street in front of the club. Sidney performs his role as Judas, nodding to the cop from above and walking away, the pitch dark night illuminated by car headlights, which also shine on Sidney's anguished face. Still to the sound of "Jam," Steve walks, carrying his guitar case, under a bridge where Kello and his partner corner him. The camera zooms from below to a close-up of Steve's anxious face. The music crescendos with a cymbal strike, and the scene shifts suddenly back to inside the club as Hamilton concludes the jam with a drum solo to the enthused applause of the crowd. Once again, the music composed by Hamilton and Katz ventures out of the club where it originated as diegetic sound and overlays the action of the film. Here, it serves to both humanize Sidney at his most despicable—for a moment before he nods to Kello he seems filled with regret—and also serves to connect Steve with an artistry and energy that seems heedless of the threat represented by Sidney and Hunsecker.

But at the same time, it does not function completely anemphatically, climaxing as it does with the exact moment Steve realizes his extreme danger. "Jam" works as both Afromodernist intervention—as the soundtrack to Steve's imminent beating, the jam he is in—and as alienation effect, with jazz almost, but not quite, oblivious to the film's narrative. Among the apparently all-white clientele in both sequences, the scholarly young aficionada at the Elysian listens attentively, and the whole crowd erupts at the end of "Jam" at Robards, as Hamilton explodes on the drums. Meanwhile, by betraying Steve, Sidney damns himself and his master, Hunsecker.

The end of the film serves up just deserts for each character, just as the Production Code required. Sidney arrives at night to Hunsecker's penthouse, brought by a call from Susan, although he thinks it was Hunsecker who summoned him. He finds the darkened apartment open, and he seems shocked by a huge Buddha head dominating the living area and even more shocked when Susan tries to commit suicide. He manages to prevent her leap from the balcony, but she sets him up with her brother regardless. Hunsecker enters the apartment to find Sidney in her bedroom, with Susan in a nightgown on the bed saying to Sidney, "Get out of here." She looks down and says nothing when Hunsecker accuses Sidney of putting his "hands on my sister." Hunsecker beats Sidney and then telephones Kello, who dutifully and gleefully shows up out on the street to finally have his way with Sidney; the last shot of Sidney shows Kello and his sidekick dragging his crumpled figure away. Up in the penthouse, Hunsecker stands behind Susan at the door as she prepares to leave. His big hands press on the door as though he will prevent her from opening it, but he does nothing. As she leaves, he stands dejected, his hands still on the door. Down on the street, Susan walks into a shaft of morning sunlight on her way to Steve. One final shot shows Hunsecker's stricken visage as he watches his most prized possession leaving, and then the camera returns to Susan walking across the city street as dawn turns into daylight.

The film allows Bernstein, not Hamilton and Katz, the last musical cues. Heavy melodramatic strings sound as Sidney gets beaten, backing off to a more gentle string melody as the camera observes Susan walking away from the apartment. The score expands and swells in typical Hollywood fashion as the final titles roll. Naremore sees film noir as "both a type of modernism . . . [with] its links to high culture, its formal and moral complexity, its disdain for classical narrative, its frankness about sex, and its increasingly critical stance towards America . . . and a type of commercial melodrama."[58] *Sweet Smell*'s relative lack of box office success and subsequent fame among film lovers likely have to do with the modernist sensibility. The story of Susan and Steve along with the Bernstein score reflect the more typical Hollywood melodramatic vision. The domination of Bernstein's score leaves jazz by the wayside, implying that just as the lovers are not really interesting compared to the corrupt white men of the narrative, the real jazz of the Chico Hamilton Quintet functions only as marginalized background to the setting in which those men make their power plays. Yet *Sweet Smell* uses the real streets of Manhattan to bolster the veracity of the narrative, and the film also uses real jazz, composed by jazzmen determined, in a move of Afromodernist subversion, to increase the cultural cachet of the form. When a black man appears as the coolest and best man in the movie, some questions are raised in the mind of the spectator. The alienation effect takes hold.

That trend continues in subsequent films noirs. In the next chapter, I look at *Elevator to the Gallows*, for which the "coolest man on the planet," to quote the jazzman in *Collateral*, composes a complete score.

CHAPTER SIX

A Paris Bar Where Miles Innovates

Life is lonely again,
And only last year
Everything seemed so sure.
Now life is awful again,
A trough full of heart
Could only be a bore.

A week in Paris will ease the bite of it.
All I care is to smile in spite of it.

MUSIC AND LYRICS BY BILLY STRAYHORN[1]

*A*BOUT FORTY MINUTES INTO *ELEVATOR TO THE Gallows (Ascenseur pour l'échafaud* 1957), femme fatale Florence Carala (Jeanne Moreau) walks into a brightly lit bar and cafe late at night, in search of her lover. Just as she opens the glass door, jazz is heard, a saxophone in conversation with a trumpet. While not exactly diegetic music, it connects visually with her entry into the club, as she strolls by men at a pinball machine and jukebox. Unlike the jazz clubs in *Out of the Past, Kiss Me Deadly,* or *Sweet Smell of Success,* this sequence does not offer an overtly legible comment on African American social activism, unless that comment comes in the form of Miles Davis's distinctive sound. Twenty-four-year-old Louis Malle's first feature film, *Elevator* features two couples and gestures toward late classic Hollywood film noir and forward to the French New Wave. Classic Hollywood film noir provides a dark but familiar outline for the older protagonists' pessimistic tale of

FIGURE 6.1. *A Paris bar*

illicit love and murder, while the careless younger couple evoke the protagonists in *Breathless* (*À bout de souffle* 1960).

Davis's jazz soundtrack both characterizes the two sets of lovers and provides the undeniable emotional connection to the femme fatale. Thirty-
year-old Miles Davis composed his first film score using music in a fairly
typical fashion, linking themes with specific characters and relying on the
expressive content of the music to explain a protagonist's state of mind.
Nevertheless, the music sometimes refuses subordination to the images.
Afromodernism appears in the integration of Davis's sound into the film.
The soundtrack exhibits a "veneer of hegemonic alignment," while also
advancing Davis's creative endeavors.[2] The jazzman's unique and innovative sound sometimes prevents the narrative from dominating and forces
the spectator to hear as well as see. The riveting visual images of Moreau
and the equally riveting aural claim upon the viewer's attention in the
form of Davis's music engender a tension-filled détente, one that exemplifies an alienation effect.

Unlike those of many of the femmes fatales of classic noir, Florence's
motivations are clear. She wants to be with her lover, Julien (Maurice
Ronet), and will have him kill her husband to achieve her goal. Malle
credits Moreau (they were also lovers at the time) with helping him figure
out how to deal with actors in his first two films.[3] She had a successful film
career in B-movies prior to *Elevator*, but the thirty-year-old Moreau cata-
pulted into focus as the star of Malle's first film and earned both praise

and media attention in his second film, *Les amants* (*The Lovers* 1958), as a wife who leaves her husband and her polo-playing Parisian lover for a handsome young archeologist who helps her when her car breaks down. According to Hugo Frey, this film supposedly provided "the first filmic representation of a female orgasm," leading to "one of the most famous trials in the history of American censorship and obscenity" and a Supreme Court judgment "that a film could only be censored for obscenity if it was of absolutely no social importance, which he [Supreme Court Justice Brenner] did not consider to be true of *Les amants*."[4] But before she portrayed a woman in the throes of physical passion, Moreau portrayed mental anguish, doubt, and desire as she walked down rain-slicked, nighttime Champs-Élysées, her face illuminated only by the lights from storefront windows. Almost no one in the world of the film can keep their eyes off her. She is the object of everyone's gaze as she purses her lips and tosses her hair, accompanied only by her occasional voice-over and the heartrending sound of Davis's trumpet.

The director cites both Robert Bresson (*Diary of a Country Priest* 1951, *A Man Escaped* 1956), with whom he had apprenticed, and Alfred Hitchcock (*Rear Window* 1954, *To Catch a Thief* 1955, *The Man Who Knew Too Much* 1956) as his inspiration.[5] With its murderous lovers, the film seems equally indebted to classic films noirs such as *Double Indemnity* (1944) and *The Postman Always Rings Twice* (1946). As I note above, critics—including Malle's collaborator, Jean-Claude Carrière—often count *Elevator* as an early or incipient film in the *nouvelle vague*, or New Wave, of young French filmmakers.[6] Like other films of the time, it includes natural lighting, subtle use of music, and attention to the mundane and sometimes brutal nature of human interactions. *Elevator*, with its jazz soundtrack, criminal older lovers, and careless, criminal young lovers brought film noir "to the mean streets of Paris" and illustrated a "sense of ennui that marked contemporary culture."[7]

Elevator propelled the already successful young collaborative filmmaker to individual fame. Malle had worked closely with Jacques-Yves Cousteau on the undersea documentary *The Silent World* (*Le monde du silence* 1956), which won both the Palme d'Or at Cannes (1956) and the Academy Award for Best Documentary Film (1957).[8] Apparently, an ear infection kept Malle from returning to work with Cousteau on his next documentary, and after a brief stint as assistant director to Robert Bresson, he started work on *Elevator*.[9] Malle collaborated with rightist novelist Roger Nimier on the screenplay, based on a crime novel a friend bought at a rail station shop.[10] According to Malle, Nimier called the book stupid; Malle countered, "Yes, but the plot is good."[11] Then, they reworked the novel to include Florence, the most memorable character in the film. While Malle and Nimier invented the character, the jazz makes people remember her.

Malle was an avid fan of the prolific innovator Davis. He had even featured a half-obscured Davis album cover in the room of one of the young protagonists, but never dared hope to include Davis in the project, when "by a bizarre coincidence, when [Malle] was editing and was about to make the choice of music, Miles Davis came to Paris."[12] Davis arrived without any of his usual musicians but had a group of talented local jazz-men: Barney Wilen on tenor saxophone, René Urtreger on piano, Pierre Michelot, and Kenny Clarke, the American bebop drummer who had recently moved to Paris and would contribute to a number of other French soundtracks as well as the soundtrack for *Odds Against Tomorrow*.

Elevator features Davis at a critical creative juncture. At the time a central figure in hard bop, as Scott Yannow explains, with its "blazing tempos," simpler melodies, and openness "to the influence of R & B," Davis had just finished recording the cool jazz classic *Miles Ahead* (1957) with Gil Evans and a nineteen-piece supporting band in the US.[13] *Elevator* signaled a new direction for the artist. Malle talks about Davis's work on the film:

> I showed him the film twice, only twice, and we agreed on the parts where we felt music was needed. And we took advantage of the one night off he had from the club. We rented a sound studio in Paris, on the Champs-Élysée and started working, as jazz musicians do, very slowly. In that one night, the whole score was recorded. . . . It's one of the very few film scores that is completely improvised. I don't think Miles Davis had had time to prepare anything. We would run those segments that we had chosen for music, and he would start rehearsing with his musicians.[14]

In his autobiography, Davis contradicts Malle, saying, "I would look at rushes of the film and get musical ideas to write down."[15] The disparity in the way Malle and Davis remember the process serves as a kind of analogue for the tension between image and sound evidenced on screen.[16] John Szwed's biography of Davis supports Davis's account and suggests the film work came up as an alternative to a cancelled tour.[17] Szwed also notes that Davis said "he'd never done anything like that, but if he liked the film, he'd try it."[18] Davis, in "devising themes for the film . . . improvised on scales instead of chords, simplifying the music harmonically and maximizing emotional content with slow drawn-out phrases—often based on nothing more than a D minor scale."[19] These modal themes provided a soundtrack for the mature lovers in the film; the music alone arouses sympathetic feelings. Royal S. Brown describes it more thoroughly as "a set of minor mode improvisations, filled with tritons and minor thirds, with Davis's trumpet wailing softly."[20] For Davis, *Elevator* inspired the modal jazz experiments that would occupy him for the next decade.

Gary Giddins discusses the amount of music, suggesting that Malle used less than half the music Davis left him with, "less than 20 minutes" in eighty-seven minutes.[21] Music accompanies less than twenty percent of the film, yet Malle asserts, "I strongly believe without Miles Davis's score the film would not have had the critical and public response that it had."[22] The music in the film resides at the absolute cutting edge of new, modern, and modal yet still manages to follow Hollywood's propensity for leitmotifs and overt emotional signposting.

The film also intentionally aims at an alienation effect, featuring a musical score that sometimes counters instead of reinforces action and characters. Malle "insisted that in *Ascenseur* the music be more important than the image in several places."[23] Mervyn Cooke suggests "Malle's intention to portray a cold and dehumanized world made the cool abstraction of Davis's modal playing singularly appropriate, and the music formed what the director termed an 'elegiac counterpoint' to the action."[24] Malle intentionally invoked an alienation effect with the improvised jazz soundtrack; critics seem to indicate they notice that alienation effect. Davis aimed for what he called abstraction. René Urtreger, the piano player, says Davis asked him "*not* to play because he wanted to improvise on the chords of 'Sweet Georgia Brown' at a very fast tempo . . . and he didn't want the original theme recognized (without piano harmony, he said, the time became a little more 'abstract')."[25] The dialogics of Davis using "Sweet Georgia Brown" but reducing it to an abstract version is a typical jazz move. Peter Watrous, discussing a recording of the music from *Elevator* but not the film, hears something else altogether. He suggests these "are some of the most gracious recordings Mr. Davis has ever made, elongated and sensuously stretched out."[26] Watrous elaborates, "They are brave: the sort of emotional exposure, where he allowed an extraordinary amount of tenderness to infuse his playing, was at odds not only with standard jazz practice, but also with conceptions of how men should express themselves."[27] The soundtrack seems at once detached and at the same time the "chilling, minimalistic notes . . . add up to so much emotion."[28] These disparate readings of Davis's music for *Elevator* add to the complexity of reading jazz, perhaps making the film a success in 1958, and certainly ensuring it still gets attention as a jazz recording. Many French jazz soundtracks followed in the late 1950s.

Jazz musicians found work in numerous French films after *Elevator*, including *Youthful Sinners* (*Les tricheurs* 1958) with music and performances by Roy Eldridge, Stan Getz, Coleman Hawkins, Sonny Stitt, and Dizzy Gillespie among others; *Dangerous Liaisons* (*Les liaisons dangereuses* 1959) starring Moreau, with music by Thelonious Monk and others and featuring Monk, Art Blakey, Lee Morgan, Wilen and Clarke (both also heard on *Elevator*), and a number of other jazzmen; and *The Road to Shame* (*Des femmes disparaissent* 1959), with music by Blakey, featuring Blakey, Morgan, and Clarke, among others. Wilen, the sax man on *Elevator*, composed and performed on *A Witness in Town* (*Un témoin dans la ville* 1959) playing with Clarke again, along with other musicians.[29]

In a fascinating aside to his analysis of the soundtrack music in *Elevator*, Morris Holbrook asserts that the tune the guard whistles as he locks the gate at Julien's building is from "Cortege," an "intertextual allusion to the celebrated dirge from *No Sun in Venice*," a film made the year before *Elevator*, and whose score by John Lewis of the Modern Jazz Quartet (MJQ) "was very much in the limelight at the time of the Davis/Malle collaboration."[30] French cinema's first use of a complete jazz score in *No Sun in Venice* predates *Elevator*, and the later film makes a sly dialogic reference to the success of the earlier score through a musical reference. Holbrook notes that both soundtracks were revolutionary—Lewis's score as the first jazz soundtrack and Davis's score as the first full-length film score to use improvisation.[31] *No Sun in Venice*, a twisted tale of crime and passion filmed in color and set in sumptuous Venice, might easily be seen as noir-influenced. The plot certainly has enough twists, although the femme fatale does not drive the narrative except by her choice of lovers, and the camera work is relatively straightforward. Lewis's Afromodernist technique of mixing classical and jazz musical styles appears in the film; with "brilliant scoring technique, Lewis managed to compose . . . [three] related pieces in such a manner that they fit together polyphonically into a fugal design."[32] Lewis's soundtrack led to "a Town Hall debut," and then "a highly acclaimed tour through . . . Europe during the last two months of 1957,"[33] and *Odds Against Tomorrow*'s soundtrack is equally complex. Nevertheless, the reference to "Cortege" from *No Sun in Venice* certainly hints that all will not end well in *Elevator*.

Elevator opens with Florence and Julien declaring their love for each other. They never appear physically together except in photographs developed in the denouement, but the narrative focus on the couple begins with these first shots, alternating close-ups of their faces engaged in a passionate telephone conversation prior to the first murder of the film. As they exchange vows of love over the phone, the trumpet begins as background music to their dialogue. As the camera pulls back to observe Julien on the phone in the window of a stark, modern office building from an ever-increasing distance, the trumpet begins to speak for them, standing in for their conversation, linking the mournful music with the lovers' desire and hopelessness. Florence ends the conversation by saying, "When it's done, drive over in your big car, pull up in front, and I'll get in next to you . . . then we'll be free." Despite the fact that Julien plans to murder the inconvenient husband (also his boss) before the end of the day, the lovers appear more resigned than nervous and excited.

Julien proceeds to kill the husband, Simon Carala (Jean Wall), an arms dealer. Accompanied by the same elegiac music as the opening sequence, he enters the foyer of Carala's office and slowly walks toward his intended victim. Julien, a paratrooper and cool-headed hero of the First Indochina War, has nothing but disdain for his lover's husband, disdain that seems as much connected to Carala's profit from France's various unpopular colonialist wars as any personal grudge. Surely Julien has profited, too, with his handsome clothes and big car. Yet as Frey notes, "the one potential hero . . . the former paratrooper . . . is shown in the film to be the victim of modern society."[34] Although "his service to France no doubt merited respect . . . the new post-war leaders (Carala the business man, the journalists from the popular press, or the absurd police officer) exploit or market him to their own commercial ends."[35] In France, the veterans of the Indochinese and later Algerian Wars were, much like the Vietnam veterans in America, disenfranchised by their service. Julien's experiences have led to a profound sense of alienation and ennui, dispelled only by his connection to his lover, Florence. He murders her husband without apparent remorse, as Davis provides the musical track that continues until interrupted by the remarkably noisy electric pencil sharpener in another office. The auditory detail evokes Hitchcock, and the sound drowns out the gunshot that kills Carala.

After the murder, Julien locks the door from the inside of the older man's office to make it look like suicide.[36] A black cat on the railing outside serves as additional notice to the spectator, if not Julien, that he is doomed. Not until he has started his car out on the street does Julien see he has left a piece of crucial evidence dangling on the outside of the building, the grappling hook and improbably thin rope he used to gain access to and egress from Carala's office foyer. He reenters the building, but before he can retrieve it, the guard whistling "Cortege" turns off the power, and Julien finds himself trapped inside the elevator in the high rise, waiting, waiting, and waiting for the law to catch him.

After Julien commits the oedipal crime of killing an older man invested with authority in order to gain access to a woman, he becomes the father

FIGURE 6.2. *The black cat*

figure in another drama. An awkward, insecure, and jealous young Louis
(Georges Poujouly) obsessed with cars decides to steal Julien's big American convertible, a Chevrolet Deluxe, left running with the keys in it on
the street. He takes his girlfriend Véronique (Yori Bertin), a flower-shop
girl with an abiding crush on Julien, for a ride. Louis and Véronique's ex-
ploits play out to a bebop theme, "a very fast set of improvisations in which
the muted trumpet is joined by the sax over rapid figures in the bass."[37]
Each time the bebop appears associated with the young couple it emphasizes their complete lack of forethought about their actions: the theft of a
car, the murder of a German couple, the stealing of another car, and even
a suicide attempt. After they take Julien's Chevy, lively bebop accompanies
their enjoyment of the convertible and the wind in Véronique's hair. Providing a subtle diegetic cue, the young woman fiddles with the radio dial,
perhaps turning the jazz down a bit, as she ransacks the car, finding Julien's
raincoat, his spy camera (which will figure in solving both murder plots),
and his gun. Louis appropriates both the raincoat and gun, while Davis's
music races along with the criminal couple through Paris traffic. Their dis-
covery of a gun in a stolen car and their carelessness with it prefigures the
events in *Breathless*, when an equally feckless car thief cavalierly shoots a
motorcycle police officer with a gun he finds in the glove box.

The young criminals in *Elevator* race against a Mercedes 300SL, a gull-
wing sports car driven by an older German, Horst Bencker (Iván Petrovich), and his attractive wife, Frieda (Elga Andersen), and are improbably

invited to join the older couple for the evening. According to Malle, the young man, Louis, represents "a new generation, . . . the *blousons noirs* because they all wore black leather, those kids from the suburbs," a French version of *The Wild One* (1953).[38] He tries to have deep thoughts, telling the cheery German tourist whom he will later shoot, "my generation has other things on its mind," as he refuses the champagne he has been offered. As he adjusts the stereo in the motel room, again playing a bop tune by Davis, Louis seems somewhat aware of war and strife outside his existence, citing "four years of occupation: Indochina, Algeria," to the self-satisfied Bencker. After a night of drinking at a strangely modern hotel, during which the German businessman repeatedly taunts the teetotaler Louis for his youth, inexperience, and Frenchness, Louis kills the German, who holds a cigar wrapper as though it is a gun muzzle, and his beautiful blond wife, who holds nothing but her dressing gown. Although he has trouble operating it, Louis steals the dead Germans' Mercedes. The young man seeks to assert his masculinity with two older men, both of whom have what he desires. He steals Julien's car, shoots Bencker and then Bencker's wife almost haphazardly, and drives away with his young girlfriend.

In all of the key scenes of Véronique and Louis, bop underscores the characters' youth and carelessness. The music changes and develops, but the style of the jazz that accompanies these sequences begins to "carry representational meaning as well."[39] Véronique and Louis remain foolish kids, and the racing scales obstruct any possible emotional attachment with them. After the two murders, the young delinquents attempt to commit suicide in Véronique's Paris apartment by taking sleeping pills. Véronique dreams of romantic headlines. She suggests they will die as the music plays on, but despite the Miles Davis album sleeve on the table behind her turntable, she puts the needle down on a classical record, "Haydn's String Quartet in F. op. 3, no. 5."[40] "We'll only be together in the headlines," she assures Louis. For Davis, the bebop thematic, like the classical soundtrack, has perhaps been overdone and no longer interests him. Ian Carr points to the "two polarities . . . in Miles's work: the quiet brooding aspect on the one hand, and the furious aggression on the other."[41] Davis's musical investment, and the spectator's, resides with the brooding modal sounds that accompany Florence and, to a lesser extent, Julien.

The two young lovers do not die; they only sleep deeply and wake up to a visit from Florence, who has tracked them down after figuring out that they are responsible for the murders being attributed to Julien. She tells them to stay put and leaves the newspaper accusing Julien of the murder of the Germans. Louis thinks he might get away with it, but his subconscious, like Julien's, sees to it that he does not. Instead of leaving town,

FIGURE 6.3. *A hint of Miles Davis on screen*

he returns to the scene of the crime on his stolen scooter to find the photographer developing the photos from Julien's little camera that prove Louis is the murderer of the Germans and that Julien and Florence are lovers and had a motive for killing Carala. The police are watching the images develop as well. The law will assert itself, sending Louis away for a double murder and Julien away for a single murder. As for Florence and the imaginative Véronique? Twenty years?

Florence has an interior monologue illuminating her thoughts, while Davis's composition illuminates her mood. No other characters enjoy the intimacy of the voice-over. Susan Hayward identifies this type of voice-over as intra-diegetic, "the inner thoughts or voices of a narrator whose story we are witnessing," and notes it allows for a "double privileging — we are positioned not only physically but also psychically as the subject."[42] And the music provides triple privileging as Florence wanders the cafe-and-street scene on a rainy Paris evening, wondering about her lover. The empathetic jazz binds the spectator to her even more. Her first interior monologue occurs as she sees the flower-shop girl go by in Julien's car, with a man at the wheel. She thinks, "He got cold feet, he couldn't pull the trigger. Coward." Internally, she calls it "shabby" that he would take up with another woman, despite that fact that she has similarly taken up with Julien. Later, Florence will acknowledge her own "cold feet," although in response to a cool night out, not to a criminal act; nevertheless, she connects herself to her lover even as she accuses him of failing her. The music connects them as well. As Florence leaves the cafe where she expected to meet Julien, walking out onto the street accompanied by a loud clap of thunder, the cymbals and piano start up, and the scene shifts to outside Julien's elevator prison as the trumpet joins in. When the camera enters the elevator to watch Julien trying various tactics to escape, the music accompanies his fiddling at first and then stops, leaving only the diegetic sound of his careful struggles with his lighter and the mechanical rollers of the contraption that has him trapped.

Florence and Julien are connected by the soundtrack as well as the music. In one sequence, Florence stands outside the locked gate of the building containing Julien and her now dead husband, shaking the metal bars of the gate. The transition to Florence reveals that Julien hears the sound from his elevator prison. At first, the diegetic tapping seems like the clacking of a typewriter somewhere on the floor to which he has a small opening. But the camera reveals that the sound Julien hears is Florence, standing outside the building, expressing her frustration with him. In a narrative aside comparable to the black cat on the railing, a little girl playing on the street questions Florence, asking, "What are you doing?" Florence tells the child to "run along home," which she does. But first the child picks up the grappling hook and rope, which have apparently fallen off the balcony railing during the storm, and takes the evidence with her. In most Hollywood films, the inclusion of the cat or the child in an early sequence of the film ensures the narrative will return to those moments and pick them up again. Instead, *Elevator* lets those incidents speak for themselves. Florence and Julien share a world that includes diegetic sound and nondiegetic music, yet they will never be together again.

They also share a Paris that in no way resembles the romantic city that serves as a setting for countless Hollywood love stories. Just as the romantic conception of a musical soundtrack has been abandoned, *Elevator* abandons the standard shots of the Eiffel Tower, or the streetlights coming up on the Champs-Élysées, a moment that Godard could not resist in *Breathless*. Instead, the film shows Paris as urban and alienated, with a glass-windowed high-rise and a motel that isolates its guests in well-furnished, individual, cubicle-like rooms filled with modern art and furnishings. Malle says, "I took care to show one of the first modern buildings in Paris. I invented a motel—there was only one motel in France and it was not near Paris. . . . I showed . . . a modern city, a world already somewhat dehumanized."[43] In this Paris, Florence will be picked up for being out at 5:00 a.m. without ID and with a man, a friend of Julien's. Roger Ebert claims the charge is prostitution; regardless, the city of love appears to insist its residents are safely off the streets at that hour.[44] The early morning roundup also affords the only glimpse of a black man the film allows. Well-dressed in a handsome suit, he sits on a bench in the police station as Florence and her male friend take a seat. He looks more exhausted than Florence—perhaps the early hour is the cause. French cinema, like Hollywood at the time, represents race casually. Jazz, however, has more time on screen.

The musical composition for Florence has time to develop fully in the now-famous sequence of her walking the streets. She has just left another club, after asking about Julien, and again a thunderclap closes the door on that establishment. As she walks down the street, her face illuminated by ambient light, everyone watches her: a large woman in a dress coat and hat, a police officer, the men in the stores. Sources differ on how cinematographer Henri Decaë filmed the sequence. Ebert suggests they "used a camera in a baby carriage," while the director's brother Vincent reports Decaë was "in a wheel chair and electricians holding battery-activated lamps."[45] Louis Malle claims the technicians working on the film rebelled about the "long tracking shots of Jeanne Moreau . . . lit only by the windows of the Champs-Élysée," fearing that Malle and Decaë would "destroy Jeanne Moreau."[46] For the director, however, the actor's "essential qualities came out: she could be almost ugly and then ten seconds later she would turn her face and be incredibly attractive."[47] And the praise the film received in the press confirmed Malle's realist impulse in how he filmed the star. As Pauline Kael suggests, Moreau's "sullen, sensual mask is just right for this limited but absorbing *policier*, set to Miles Davis's music."[48]

As Florence shakes her hair, strokes her face, checks out the parked automobiles for Julien's car, and finally comes to a stop to gaze blankly into a store window, Davis's trumpet accompanies her, assuring the spectator's emotional attachment. In an oft-quoted description, jazz critic Phil Johnson calls the music, "the loneliest trumpet sound you will ever hear . . . hear it and weep."[49] Despite the fact that she has obviously conspired to murder her husband, Florence receives sympathy and understanding, with the spectator's perspective on the character regulated by the voiceover and jazz that accompany her walking meditation. Four sequences feature Florence looking everywhere for Julien on the nighttime streets, sometimes in rain, asking after him in cafes and bars, one of which I mention at the beginning of the chapter, with the sounds of Davis's trumpet occasionally accompanying her. For Krin Gabbard, the street-walking sequences serve as the only time where "the music really transform[s] the images on the screen . . . when . . . Florence . . . slowly walks through the Paris night while Davis and his quintet read her mind with improvisations."[50] Although the sequences receive praise from film critics and schol-

FIGURE 6.4. *A sublime mix of cinema and sound*

ars and jazz critics, Jean-Louis Ginibre writes in *Jazz Magazine* that *Elevator* "would have remained a relatively minor film without the music of Miles Davis."[51] Davis, however, complained about Moreau's walk, saying, "The bitch didn't know how to walk in rhythm."[52]

I would counter that her walk came first, but Davis's creativity in composing for *Elevator* led him to further musical innovation. Gabbard suggests writing for these specific moments in the film may have inspired "Davis's idea of creating improvisations free of conventional song structures at the *Kind of Blue* session."[53] Ginibre, too, asserted the film "marks a decisive turning point in the work of Miles Davis."[54] Carr sees the music on *Milestones*, Davis's next album, furthering the initial concepts from *Elevator* and even, occasionally, quoting from it.[55] And most important to this discussion, Gabbard seems to consider what I have called the alienation effect in his discussion of the film music, noting:

> On one level, the music Davis created for the film gestures toward codes that were already well established in the history of film music. . . . On the other hand, the music is completely faithful to the jazz idiom. Those who know the music can hear the improvised solos and group interactions that only Miles Davis could create.[56]

Gabbard understands how the music both fulfills the requirements of a good soundtrack, allowing the narrative to dominate, and asks or allows the spectator to engage in a more nuanced reading of what is seen, and especially heard, on screen. The music in the film serves to cement the narrative connection between the lovers and emphasize their ennui.

Elevator ends in complete exhaustion, perhaps implying film noir has run its course. It is a postwar narrative translated into French, using the colonial conflicts that occupied France after World War II as an explanation for the weariness that affects the narrative. Like the American offering of Touch of Evil (1958), Elevator sees film noir to its logical conclusion—not even the good guys are good. If classic film noir once featured a hard-boiled American male protagonist whose individualist ethics ensured our identification with him, this late French noir-inspired film features a reserved and war-weary hero whose ethical choices include adultery and murder. The femme fatale, like many of her cinematic antecedents, seeks to escape her lot in life and is willing to murder to do it. Most of the dangerous women of classic film noir manipulate men to ensure their financial if not sexual independence. Florence seeks at least sexual fulfillment. While men often remain peripheral but necessary to the deadly femme fatale's desires, Julien is all Florence wants. Elevator's characters have no chance of escaping their social situations except by going to jail. The youthful criminals have no more energy to devote to the future than do the middle-aged lovers, and both couples will find that their efforts, however casual and thoughtless or carefully planned, lead nowhere. Handsome and war-weary, beautiful and frustrated, young and clueless—no one gets away with murder here. The competent protagonist of the narrative makes a stupid mistake after committing an almost perfect murder, and the youthful second murderer, with less life experience, proves even more inept. Although the film casts light on the dissatisfactions and frustrations of the sons, the murderers themselves ensure the law of the father is upheld though their ineptitude. In the end, like many films noirs, Elevator promises to punish the women more than the men who commit the murders. And even the police detective, with a face like a sleepy French Robert Mitchum, seems infected by lethargy as he solves the crimes.

The only productive energy in the narrative comes from the music. Davis manages to quote from jazz's musical past, just as the film quotes from film noir's cinematic history. Aggressive and impressive flights of bebop trumpet flourishes end in the same foolish quagmire that stops Louis and Véronique's crime spree. Yet Davis's muted trumpet "seems to penetrate every scene, holding it all together," and was acclaimed by French and other reviewers.[57] The jazz soundtrack accompanies Elevator's characters and the film's noir stylistics toward their negation. In the final sequence of the film, Davis's trumpet cues as Florence watches the photo-

FIGURE 6.5. *The lovers, together*

graphs of her and Julien together, smiling, come into being under the developing fluid. The detective tells her that Julien will get ten years for the murder of her husband, and only serve five, but that the jury will not go so easily on her, while Davis plays on. Florence's voice-over acknowledges that she will be old from now on, but at least she and her lover are together in the photos, despite the time that she expects to serve for her crime. The image of them together fades to black, as a single trumpet note plays. Only the modal jazz contributed by Davis makes it out alive.

Jazz did not kill film noir, but the contributions of jazz composers such as Davis and Ellington came at the exact moment that color, wide screens, small screens, and the momentary misguided optimism of the early 1960s nudged the black-and-white ambiguity of classic film noir from the screens, leaving jazz to make its way on its own. And while film noir had all but run its course, the jazz innovations of Davis were just midstream; he could "legitimately claim to have changed music six or seven times" with his "most radical innovations" coming "in the late 1960s."[58] Davis's interest in film composing was peripheral to his jazz artistry, yet his first soundtrack reveals an alienation effect, with the music committed to the visual but obliging attention to the aural.

Duke Ellington's and Billy Strayhorn's first soundtrack reveals even less commitment to the visual—without abandoning Hollywood's notions of film music—as we will see next.

CHAPTER SEVEN

"All the Very Gay Places"

ELLINGTON AND STRAYHORN SWING IN NORTHERN MICHIGAN

I used to visit all the very gay places,
Those come what may places
Where one relaxes on the axis
Of the wheel of life
To get the feel of life
From jazz and cocktails.

MUSIC AND LYRICS BY BILLY STRAYHORN[1]

*T*HE ROADHOUSE WHERE DUKE ELLINGTON SITS AT the piano while some of his band members play jazz, a room full of white patrons dancing and drinking, does seem like a gay place, at least until Biegler (James Stewart) hauls Laura (Lee Remick) out of the bar and berates her with a list of restrictions designed to contain her sexuality. As Biegler gets up to confront Laura, Ellington gets a short speaking part, saying to the lawyer cum jazzman, "You're not splitting the scene, man? I mean, you're not cutting out?" The sequence opens with the sound of jazz, a version of a tune called "Happy Anatomy," and the camera reveals a small jazz quintet featuring Ellington, band members Ray Nance on trumpet, Jimmy Hamilton on tenor sax, Jimmy Woode on bass, and Jimmy Johnson on drums. Later, as Biegler does cut out to apply the corrective to Laura, Pie Eye (Ellington) says "OK" in response to Biegler's "See you later, Pie Eye." The club is a rustic log venue with a big front porch and window, through which the band can be seen as Biegler guides Laura outside (figure 1.1). It seems completely unlikely that a little bar in northern Michigan, in the mythical Iron City, much less Ishpeming or Marquette, would have a jazz quintet featuring musicians such as Elling-

FIGURE 7.1. *Duke Ellington in a northern Michigan roadhouse*

ton and Nance et al., but that apparent oddity receives no notice from the film's characters.

Perhaps the audience took no notice either. Jazz was getting more and more common in movie soundtracks at the time, however. Just as jazz musicians found film scoring opportunities in France, jazz was popular in the underground movie scene in the United States. Hollywood actor and independent filmmaker John Cassavetes hired bass player and jazz-innovator Charles Mingus to score his film *Shadows* (1959), although, as Gary Giddins notes, "Mingus never completed a single arrangement for the film."[2] Giddins adds that "David Amram and Freddie Redd created famous scores for *Pull My Daisy* (1959) and *The Connection*" (1962), the former a thirty-minute beat film written and narrated by Jack Kerouac, and the latter a film about junkies, featuring Redd and saxophone-virtuoso Jackie McClean in the cast.[3] Hollywood wanted to capitalize, safely, on the jazz trend. This provided an opportunity for Ellington to work in Hollywood, a year after the release of *Elevator to the Gallows*, as the master composer, arranger, pianist, and bandleader approached sixty. David Butler details the racism that likely kept Ellington from working in Hollywood sooner, although he was eager to do so for *The Man with the Golden Arm*.[4] Instead, Elmer Bernstein composed the jazz-inflected score for that film, as he would for *Sweet Smell of Success*. Butler also notes that Ellington's music "was not so obviously rooted in a noir sensibility . . . [since] the Ellington band was defined more through its warmth, joyousness, and lyricism."[5] Ellington and his arranger and co-composer William Thomas "Billy" Strayhorn's original music begins before the main titles of the opening credits and provides the soundtrack for *Anatomy of a Murder* (1959). As I note above, Ellington appears briefly on screen, although not Strayhorn.

Ellington's music had also never been heard as a complete soundtrack in a film before. Some internet sources list *The Asphalt Jungle* (1950) as his first complete score, but Miklós Rózsa composed that score. Although only Ellington appears in the credits of *Anatomy*, he certainly wrote the music in close collaboration with Strayhorn. As record producer Irving Townsend notes, "Billy [Strayhorn] has written parts of every album we've done, sometimes in the form of entire pieces, sometimes as in the case of . . . *Anatomy* . . . short passages interwoven with the whole."[6] Strayhorn and Ellington had just completed composing *Such Sweet Thunder* (1957), inspired by Shakespeare's work, and the *Queen's Suite*, inspired by Queen Elizabeth II whom Ellington had recently met. In his autobiography, Ellington says about Strayhorn, "but it all boiled down to the same thing whether he was there or not. . . . He was always my consultant."[7] David Hajdu notes that Strayhorn went to Michigan before Ellington arrived, living with the cast and crew at "the Marquette Mather Inn . . . where Strayhorn stayed while he watched rehearsals, jotting notes for the music by day and reading Voelker's novel over sips of cognac in the hotel lounge through the evening."[8] Chris Fujiwara confirms that Strayhorn arrived in Michigan in March, with Ellington following in late April. Many of the principals comment on the cold; Fujiwara quotes Preminger's wife, Hope, saying, "It was 32 below zero, and it stayed 32 below zero almost the whole time."[9] I grew up in northern Minnesota, and I suspect it might have warmed a bit but trust it felt at least that cold to the California dwellers. When Ellington arrived, he and Stewart played piano duets together, with Stewart saying, "I never sounded so good."[10] Ellington goes on to say that once they were back in Hollywood, Preminger gave Strayhorn and him "a penthouse apartment that had seven rooms, three baths, and a patio twice as big as the apartment. . . . We spent almost the entire time there partying, enjoying ourselves and . . . the scenery. . . . Finally one day, a guy from the studio calls up and says, 'You know, Mr. Ellington, we are recording Friday.'"[11] The composers finalized the music quickly, in "about forty-eight hours."[12]

Strayhorn is never identified by name in Richard Griffith's 1959 book about the making of the film, though he appears in a photo with Preminger, film editor Louis R. Loeffler, and Ellington, looking at a section of film.[13] Much has been written about Strayhorn and Ellington's almost three-decade partnership, during which Ellington's organization paid many of Strayhorn's bills and Strayhorn often got little or no credit for his contributions.[14] The men had, according to Hajdu, an "uncommonly personal business relationship," one that resonates with a relationship between two characters in *Anatomy*, Biegler and his friend McCarthy.[15] For *Anatomy*, Ellington claims he was surprised the music was award-winning since "it really hadn't an outstanding melody to hang on to . . . [and] it wasn't done with the intention of trying to get a tune out of it. . . . I was trying to do background music fittingly."[16]

Richard Domek provides insight into the *Anatomy* score, how Strayhorn and Ellington collaborated, and how the music works on its own. Domek details two primary themes in the soundtrack: "Flirtibird," written by Ellington, and "Polly," composed by Strayhorn. Domek notes that the "Polly theme, composed by . . . Strayhorn, appears in the film even more often than the Flirtibird theme."[17] He clarifies that the "copyright for the tune known as 'Polly' . . . was registered posthumously in 1994" to Strayhorn, although it had first been registered "under Ellington's name."[18] For Domek and others, the "music as well as the entire conception of the . . . score stands as a high point of . . . the Ellington-Strayhorn process of collaboration and creation."[19] The men often collaborated from a distance, using the phone to have detailed conferences on the music they were composing.[20] Preminger's insistence on location creation provided the men with time together in Michigan, and later they enjoyed time together in California.

Because of the Afromodernist impulse to both produce Hollywood soundtracks and pursue their own musical agenda, the jazz Ellington and Strayhorn created for *Anatomy* demonstrates an alienation effect. According to Domek, the music also demonstrates "Ellington's and Strayhorn's individualistic and detailed attention to harmony and scoring practices and avoidance of more common clichés that inform the identifiable sound, the 'Ellington effect.'"[21] They did not want to sound like typical jazzy film music used in clichéd ways, or, if we believe Domek, like typical Ellington. Ellington had just had unprecedented success at the Newport Jazz Festival in 1956 and had seen his career reignited. As Ellington said, "I was born at the Newport Jazz Festival on July 7, 1956."[22] Certainly Preminger hoped to capitalize on the Ellington effect and, to an extent, had success.

Just as Mackendrick did in *Sweet Smell of Success*, Preminger had used a jazz-inflected Elmer Bernstein soundtrack in *The Man with the Golden Arm* (1955), which featured Shorty Rogers and His Giants in place of the Chico Hamilton Quintet. Butler discusses how in *The Man with the Golden Arm*, "tensions surrounding Hollywood's use of jazz" appear in the film, with "jazz as the sound of [main character] Frankie's addiction."[23] The narrative also "portrays successful jazz musicians as demanding high standards" and "acknowledges that jazz requires . . . proficiency and skill to be played well."[24] Frankie (Frank Sinatra), an aspiring jazz drummer, is also a heroin addict, and the film provided Preminger with further opportunities to fight the Production Code Administration (PCA). The director chafed against Hollywood censorship and proved instrumental in disempowering the PCA's influence in the 1950s. He released the sex comedy *The Moon Is Blue* (1953) without the PCA's seal of approval, and the film's success without the seal helped diminish the PCA's power. The director continued the fight against censorship with *The Man with the Golden Arm*, which also screened at major chains without the PCA seal.

Although Preminger had already released two films without the seal of approval, on *Anatomy* he worked closely with Geoffrey Shurlock, the head of the administration after the retirement of Joseph Breen in 1954. Shurlock and Preminger's letters about the film stay polite. Shurlock suggests, "The references to 'sperm,' 'sexual climax,' 'penetration,' etc., seem to us to be hardly suitable in a picture to be released indiscriminately for mixed audiences."[25] A subsequent letter confirms the content of a phone discussion and has Shurlock detailing the language that must be changed, such as omitting "knocked up," changing "sperm" to "evidence," and reducing "the quantitative use of the words 'rape' and 'panties.'"[26] Shurlock closes with, "Thanks again for your cooperation in dealing with this somewhat tricky problem."[27] Preminger follows up with a defense of the use of the word "penetration," responding to Shurlock's request it be replaced by "violation." He includes "some research" provided by *Anatomy of a Murder* book author, Robert Traver, who "is actually John Voelker, Justice of the Supreme Court of Michigan."[28] The research, a memorandum, includes quotes from various legal statutes, *Black's Law Dictionary*, and *Tiffany's Criminal Law*, among others. The epistolary discussion continues regarding the word "penetration"; Shurlock stands by his original request but ends his letter with a friendly, "aside from this minor annoyance, I trust that everything is going along swimmingly with the picture," and "kindest regards as always."[29] The script was changed, using "violation" and "completion" instead of "penetration." Panties, however, remain a major plot point.

Preminger's careful arguing of his case to the PCA hints at his legal background. Preminger's "father was the attorney-general of the Austro-Hungarian Empire," and as a young man the director "studied law at the University of Vienna."[30] Preminger used courtroom sequences in many of his films, including *Angel Face* (1953), *The Court-Martial of Billy Mitchell* (1955), and *Saint Joan* (1957). Preminger also availed himself of the law to assert his rights, suing Chicago mayor Richard D. Daley to ensure *Anatomy* could be screened there despite Daley's attempt to ban the film because of his objections to the film's frank discussion of rape, intercourse, and panties.[31]

Other legal actions by Preminger included the director bringing "an injunction against Columbia Pictures Corp. and Screen Gems Inc. to prevent them from interrupting the film [*Anatomy*] when it was televised," a case he lost, and an instance in the 1990s (Preminger died in 1986) when "Preminger Films threatened to sue Universal Pictures because Universal's poster for the 1995 film *Clockers* bore a 'striking resemblance' to Saul Bass's stylized design for *Anatomy*... caus[ing] Universal to change the design of the *Clockers* poster."[32] Remarkably, despite the explicit language, *Anatomy* gained the PCA seal of approval.

Some sources identify *Anatomy* as film noir but make no mention of the jazz soundtrack.[33] Despite the courtroom drama and mostly rural northern Michigan setting of the film, jazz infuses the black-and-white cinematography and ambiguous narrative with noir colorings. Fujiwara suggests, "Ellington's music, in floating above the film and only rarely pinning itself to the images... expresses... the extended context of the drama in three dimensions, temporal, geographical, and moral."[34] The lack of clarity in the morality of the characters suits late film noir. The music detaches itself from the unsolvable, unknowable circumstances, occasionally stepping up to comment briefly on the proceedings with a uniquely modern flair that plays with the more prosaic use of jazz to indicate the threat of sexuality and the dangers of the urban realm.

The film opens with a trumpet (played by Clark Terry) calling wah-wah and a blank gray screen. Saul Bass's modern titles, almost a stylistic transect of Matisse and Mondrian, promoted many Preminger productions, such as *The Man with the Golden Arm* and *Saint Joan*. Bass would go on to do art direction as well, storyboarding the shower scene in *Psycho* (1960) and the opening dance sequence in *West Side Story* (1961). For *Anatomy*, a cutout body assembles on screen, and then individual body parts take up the whole screen. For Fujiwara, "the titles indicate that the film is mainly concerned with the community, represented as a 'body.'"[35] And the soundtrack of the community finally joins into the title sequence, with a swinging orchestra developing the tune "Anatomy of a Murder." After Ellington's credit, this lively theme takes over, and the credits continue, with body parts sliding onto the screen only to be cut into pieces. Bass's credit sequence, as Leo Goldsmith details, "provides some witty juxtapositions of titles and images: James Stewart naturally gets the head; Lee Remmick [*sic*] a leg; Duke an arm: Preminger's credit comes once a disembodied hand seems to cover the lens."[36]

The music continues, without missing a beat, as the action commences. The camera watches as a man, the casually dressed former district attorney Paul Biegler (James Stewart), drives a Pontiac Chieftain convertible into the small town of Iron City at dusk. As the big car rolls down the main street, a barkeep smoking on the street waves at the driver, walks back into an almost empty club and lets a man (Arthur O'Connell) drinking at the bar know, "Your pal just drove into town." The man, Parnell McCarthy, an out-of-work lawyer, asks with an air of polite but sad desperation for one more drink and notes he will have to pay for it tomorrow. The barman pours him another, treating him gently.

Meanwhile, Biegler continues home. He pulls up in front of a two-story darkened house, walks into the entryway, turns on lights as he goes, hangs up his creel and fishing vest, goes into the kitchen, turns on the water in the sink, dumps three fish into the sink, and lays out newspaper and wax paper. Then he walks out of the kitchen to call a potential client, while the water still runs in the kitchen. During this whole sequence, the same lively jazz piece is carried over from the credits. This extradiegetic music does not stop until Biegler dials the operator and she answers. The various instruments then give way to just a few bars of piano music by Ellington, three notes repeated to point to the crucial importance of the call, and the opening of the narrative proper. But the opening is again deferred, as the return from fishing served as a deferral, since the phone operator does not know when the party Biegler seeks, the wife of a murder suspect, will return.

In many classic films noirs, the streets at dusk would glisten wetly with rain while the man in his car searches desperately for answers; usually this would not happen in his house at the kitchen sink. The house in which Biegler lives is the Ishpeming home and birthplace of Traver/Voelker who wrote the novel *Anatomy of a Murder*. As Traver, Voelker also wrote *Trout Magic* and *Trout Madness: Being a Dissertation on the Symptoms and Pathology of this Incurable Disease by One of Its Victims*, both books published by Simon and Schuster in 1989, and at least three other books on fishing, an obsession the character Biegler shares. The particularized mise-en-scène in the two-story house speaks to the potential richness of location shooting and provides a detailed characterization for the protagonist. He has lived in the house his whole life and has his office there. A note from his secretary gets stuck through by deer antlers near the front door; a repeated pattern of pine boughs adorns the wallpaper; inexpensively framed diplomas hang in the study; and an upright piano stands against the wall. It shocked me to see his friend, McCarthy, stub out a cigarette on the frame of the kitchen door later in the opening sequence, but a black smudge already marks the spot, and Biegler does not pause in his fish cleaning. The low-key lighting of the opening sequence evokes film noir—wall lamps create pools of light—but all that is obscured in the shadows is the specific but unremarkable details of a northern Michigan family home, now a bachelor pad that accommodates the country lawyer's office.

In an essay about Preminger, Christian Keathley notes that Preminger addressed "controversial social issues (sexual affairs, drug abuse, homosexuality) head on.... The social issues under interrogation in Preminger's films were not subtextual—they were manifest content."[37] In *Anatomy*, the manifest content includes murder, rape, assault, suspected incest, and a criminal trial. Yet the whole film was shot on location in Michigan, and all the settings—including the courthouse, various roadhouses, the lawyer's house, and even the fish and the kitchen sink—receive ample and detailed screen time. Keathley suggests "working on individual scenes and shots— moments that strike us, that perplex us, that gently call our attention to the fact they are *like that*—may be the best approach [to Preminger]."[38] The subdued but intriguing opening gambit, with two friends drinking and talking law into the evening, does seem like a classic film noir. And Ellington's sophisticated music cues the spectator that crime, ambiguity, and a femme fatale will appear.

She appears when Mrs. Manion (Lee Remick) calls Biegler back, just over eight minutes into the film. The phone rings, interrupting the comfortable teasing banter of Biegler and McCarthy, as Biegler tinkles the piano keys. As the operator connects Laura Manion to Biegler, loud discordant jazz bursts out from the phone, making it hard for the characters to hear each other. The music at first appears diegetic, perhaps issuing from a jukebox or band out of sight in the club where Mrs. Manion places her call, but as Biegler covers the mouthpiece so he and McCarthy can discuss him taking the case, the volume stabilizes and it becomes nondiegetic background music, introducing the "Flirtibird" theme that accompanies the character. She certainly looks the femme fatale—dark sunglasses although she telephones from a roadhouse at night, a trench coat belted at the waist, and Muffy, a lively, furry terrier. She compliments Biegler, telling him he's "been so highly recommended," and begs him to take her husband's case. McCarthy encourages Biegler to take the case. He takes the compliment and agrees to meet Laura Manion and her jailed husband in the morning.

Jazz also accompanies the morning meeting. As Laura leans against her car, longtime Ellington band member Johnny Hodges's saxophone voices approval with a wolf-whistle glissando, as the camera circles and zooms in. Ellington notes in an interview, "I saw the rushes the first Sunday in Ishpeming and then the minute I saw her there leaning against that car I knew I was on the right track with my Number 1 theme of 'Flirty bird' [Flirtibird on the soundtrack] . . . It was a thing with her eyes and she

FIGURE 7.2. *"Take the case."*

FIGURE 7.3. *Mrs. Manion*

absolutely appeared to be, you know, sort of flirting all the time which would easily be mistaken by someone and it was."[39] Still in dark glasses, but now dressed in slacks and a snug V-necked sweater, Laura shakes Biegler's hand, introduces her dog, and compliments the lawyer again, sizing him up and saying, admiringly, "You're tall," recalling for noir enthusiasts both the novel and the film *The Big Sleep*. The *Anatomy* novel apparently calls for a supremely attractive but older woman, and Preminger originally cast Lana Turner, then in her mid-thirties, but she withdrew over a costume dispute with Preminger. Remick, twenty-four at the time, earned

FIGURE 7.4. *The cigarette-holder*

the role and plays Laura as a confident sex kitten, although her real desires remain hidden or are not the concern of the narrative. By Laura's own admission, she was recently raped and beaten by Quill, after which her husband went to Quill's bar and shot him five times. As with all the characters in *Anatomy*, Laura's motivations and her past experiences remain ambiguous. We never know what happened between her and Quill or between her husband and her. Is the black eye she covers with dark glasses the result of Quill's beating, as she claims, or from her husband?

Ben Gazzara plays Laura's husband, Frederick "Manny" Manion, a Korean War veteran. Gazzara, in his late twenties at the time, plays Manion as abrasive, handsome, and masculine; he is also not particularly tall. Pinkerton describes him as "pompous, with his ivory cigarette holder; remote; darkly thoughtful; and quick to anger."[40] The cigarette-holder serves as one of those bits of "actor's business—the physical activities they are engaged in while talking."[41] Manion acts supremely disdainful of Biegler, at least initially, and uninterested in the criminal process. His military fatigues and macho façade seem incongruent with the graceful cigarette-holder, which for me evokes wealthy older women and health concerns. Manion's hypermasculinity masks insecurities, and the film advertises the weakness of his façade with a delicately phallic compensatory object. Manion uses the holder throughout a conversation with Biegler, and the lawyer graciously ignores the addition to Manion's smoke, although he borrows Manion's lighter and smokes a cigar as they talk. The cigar signals secure masculinity, whereas the cigarette-holder seems to signal less than that.

Yet Biegler does not have the kind of relationships with women that a secure heterosexual man in a Hollywood movie generally has. In *Civilization and Its Discontents*, Sigmund Freud asserts that sublimation allows the individual to channel potentially destructive pyschosexual energy into socially productive activities, "shifting the instinctual aims in such a way that they cannot come up against frustrations from the external world."[42] In the film, McCarthy notes that Biegler's frustration with not being re-elected after many years as public prosecutor constitutes a painful rejection by the body politic, one McCarthy sees Biegler drowning out with jazz, fancy cigars, whiskey, and women—wait, I mean fishing. A man can certainly fish now and then, but the opening sequence reveals the extent to which Biegler catches, cleans, and relentlessly stores fish in his refrigerator. When his secretary Maida Rutledge (Eve Arden) arrives the next morning, McCarthy snores on the couch—he apparently sleeps over frequently—while Biegler reads the newspaper at the kitchen table. She opens the fridge to put away the milk and can barely find room for the bottle; countless waxed paper packages of fish fill the shelves. Perhaps the character's inability to eat or to give away his catch speaks to a desire to hold onto his modest angling success, to assert control when things seem out of his hands. Biegler has been sublimating his anger and frustration about not productively serving the public. His work may itself have been a successful sublimation of sexual energy that could not find an outlet in an acceptable heterosexual union.

The bachelor's closest relationship appears to be with McCarthy, another man who also nurses (with drink instead of fishing) deep psychic

FIGURE 7.5. *The refrigerator*

FIGURE 7.6. *Hard-boiled eggs and a personal business relationship*

wounds. McCarthy has the sympathy and understanding of the barkeeper and the love and understanding of Biegler. Like Ellington and Strayhorn, Biegler and McCarthy have "an uncommonly personal business relationship," and like Strayhorn, McCarthy drowns his discontents in alcohol.[43] As Krin Gabbard suggests, "in both cases we have a tall, piano-playing man and an alcoholic sidekick who love each other and are in many ways co-dependent."[44] After Biegler has met with both the Manions, but before he agrees to take the case, he and McCarthy meet to eat hard-boiled eggs together at an outdoor lunch counter in a rail yard on the waterfront. The distinctive mise-en-scène—a crane moves back and forth high overhead in the background, apparently swinging from nowhere to nowhere, in tune with the give and take of the dialogue as McCarthy convinces Biegler to help Manion come up with his defense—evokes a strange sort of dehumanized and mechanized environment, located outside the rural but not quite urban either. The bits of actors' business—the peeling and eating of the eggs, the passing of the salt, all without background music of any sort—cement the fondness, respect, and warmth between the two men and belie the peculiar and discordant setting, pointing to the importance of their connection. Later in the film, Biegler overtly states his devotion to McCarthy; indeed, he and Maida instigate a care-filled intervention, successfully diverting his alcoholism into productive work during the murder trial and, at the end of the film, into work as Biegler's law partner. Gabbard astutely comments that collaborators Ellington and Strayhorn wrote "music that was a curious complement to Stewart's unique [bisexual] persona."[45] Although the novel ends with the suggestion of a romance between the lawyer and Quill's daughter, the film omits that possibility, and Biegler remains a bachelor, his ambiguous persona intact.

Stewart's unique, sexually ambiguous persona also appears in the famous *Rear Window* (1954), in which he plays Jeff, a photographer temporarily confined to a wheelchair by a work-related injury. He practically ignores his luminous girlfriend, Lisa, played by Grace Kelly, as she attempts to seduce him with beautiful dresses, fine food, and even a silky dressing gown. Stewart's characters are always much less overtly masculine than other actors', such as John Wayne's, yet Stewart, not Wayne, gets the sought-after woman in *The Man Who Shot Liberty Valance* (1962). In *Anatomy*, Laura's self-aware and powerful acknowledgment of her ability to attract men flusters Biegler profoundly. One sequence takes place in his home office. He arrives late to find Laura comfortably stretched out on his couch, still wearing her sunglasses, which hide a black eye, apparently having listened to all of his albums, "from Dixieland to Brubeck," according to his secretary Maida.[46] In any case, Biegler interviews Laura about her background and the assault that precipitated her husband's shooting of Quill. First, he turns down the Dixieland version of "Happy Anatomy," an Ellington original tune that appears three times in the film.

In the course of the interview, Biegler asks Laura if she was afraid of her soon-to-be attacker as he drove her home from his bar. She says "not really," since men are always interested in her and even Biegler is interested. He counters, saying he is only interested in helping her husband. She responds that she knows the lawyer would not try anything, but she can tell by the way he looks at her that he is interested. Biegler defends

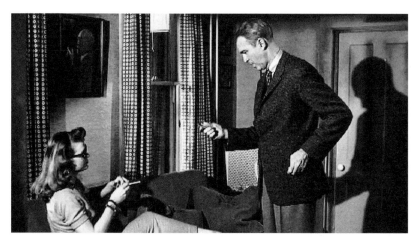

FIGURE 7.7. *Laura at Biegler's home office*

himself, saying it would be pretty hard not to look at her. Laura acknowledges her supposedly provocative wardrobe—no girdle, a tight sweater and slacks, shoes with kitten heels, and asks, "Don't you like it?" Biegler responds, "I love it; I just love it," and then reins in his obvious discomfort by insisting the conversation return to the case.

As I note in chapter 1, Biegler will rein in Laura's wardrobe and behavior during the trial. She complies to the best of her abilities. Biegler is not immune to Laura's feminine charm; nevertheless, his true attachments remain to his friend McCarthy, to his legal cases, to fishing, and to jazz. Unlike fishing, which figures strongly in both the novel and film, jazz appears just once in the novel, which suggests Biegler plays drums, not piano. In the novel, Biegler "stops off at the Halfway House for one tall drink, just one . . . .[and] by midnight, having bought my way into the jazz combo, that old hepcat Polly Biegler and his borrowed fly-swatters was making crazy on the drums."[47]

Manion's case eventually comes to the trial phase, and the courtroom sequences feature no music at all. Just as *Anatomy*'s location shooting lends an atmosphere of concrete reality to the narrative, during the trial, the benevolent but no-nonsense Judge Weaver seems equally anchored in the real world. Weaver is played by Joseph N. Welch, a lawyer and special counsel for the army in the Army-McCarthy hearings; the neophyte actor earned a nomination from the Golden Globes for best supporting actor, and from the British Academy Film Awards for most promising newcomer at nearly sixty years of age.[48] Sadly, Welch died just a year later. But as with Ellington, the famous lawyer also provided a marketing coup for Columbia and Preminger. Audiences recognized Welch as the lawyer who in 1954 challenged Senator Joseph McCarthy on television screens across the country, saying to McCarthy after a particularly vicious attack on one of Welch's young associates, "Until this moment, Senator, I think I never really gauged your cruelty or your recklessness. . . . Let us not assassinate this lad further, Senator. You have done enough. Have you no sense of decency, sir, at long last? Have you left no sense of decency?"[49] Debate swirls about whether this exchange, or the televised hearings, or general weariness for McCarthy's tactics led to the senator's downfall, but Welch earned some of the credit and a seat on the bench in a Hollywood movie.

In *Sweet Smell of Success* the implications of the paranoid environment created by the House Un-American Activities Committee (HUAC) hearings remain subtext; here, the film celebrates the demise of the communist witch hunt by putting a public hero perceived as ending the hearings on screen. Welch insisted on a part for his wife, Agnes, who earned a role as a juror, and as Griffith notes, "Welch wound up with one of the high-

FIGURE 7.8. *Judge Weaver and the lawyers discuss panties*

est salaries in the film," a gamble that paid dividends in "that amount of coverage given to the casting in newspapers, magazines, and television."[50] Griffith goes on to claim the courtroom spectators were chosen "primarily for their faces, from the ranks of the unemployed," indicating Preminger practiced his own version of typage, where nonprofessional actors are cast according to external traits that represent a class.[51]

In addition to Welch, Remick, and Ellington, another relative new-comer to the big screen, George C. Scott, plays the assistant state attorney general, Claude Dancer. In one brilliant courtroom sequence, the young and aggressive Mr. Dancer, dark-haired and dressed in a dark suit, questions Laura. Dancer effectively blocks Biegler's view of his witness as he manages to make her less and less comfortable. With Biegler leaning left and then right to make sure he can see Laura, presumably to offer her support, Dancer almost seems to have eyes in back of his head, his threatening form taking up all the space between Biegler and Laura. Dancer seems well-aware that Biegler's folksy displays of humor, anger, and his self-effacing asides are powerful tactics. Scott, as Dancer, brings a skeptical, voracious quality to the state's pursuit of justice.

As with the film in the script phase, panties get attention in the trial phase. After Quill attacked her, Laura cannot find her panties, which she says he ripped off of her. When Biegler gets the alleged rape admitted as a possible motive, requiring a discussion of the incident, Judge Weaver calls the lawyers to the bench to consider another word for panties, which he finds carries a "light connotation." Biegler claims bachelorhood. The prosecutor says that is what his wife always calls them, and Dancer says he learned a French word during his time overseas but is "afraid that might be slightly suggestive." Weaver agrees, "most French words are," and tells the jury and courtroom audience about the panties so they can get their snickers out of the way. He goes on to say that there is nothing funny about "a pair of panties that led to the violent death of one man and the possible incarceration of another." Or the violation of a woman, I would add.

Later, while questioning Laura, Dancer tells her, "I'm quite concerned about the panties." He is also concerned that, although Laura says the items were nylon with lace up the side and have a label from "the Smart Shop in Phoenix," she cannot recall if they were white or pink. She does admit she does not always wear panties, after some goading by Dancer. Later, Quill's adult daughter will find the torn panties in the laundry of the hotel she runs, where Quill and she both live, proving Quill took the panties from the scene of Laura's violation. For Maria Pramaggiore, her missing panties stand in for "the fact that Laura's personhood is nowhere to be found"; she is absent "as a subject of anything but male fantasy."[52] She seems secure in her ability to attract male attention, but little else. As Pramaggiore suggests, "her rape is deemed less important than her husband's reputation."[53] Of course, her husband is on trial for murder. Despite the tenacious prosecution, Manion is found not-guilty by the jury, who buy Biegler and Manion's assertion that he killed Quill under the grip of an irresistible impulse, or temporary insanity.

Noir inconspicuously infuses *Anatomy*. Eve Arden's character Maida Rutledge has the same last name as Lauren Bacall's character in *The Big Sleep* (1946), and Arden played Ida, the best friend of Mildred (Joan Crawford) in *Mildred Pierce* (1945). Laura's comment about Biegler's height recalls an in-joke from *The Big Sleep*. Private detective Philip Marlowe, as written by Raymond Chandler in the novel, is described as tall. Marlowe as played by Humphrey Bogart required a change in dialog with Martha Vickers, playing Vivian Rutledge's (Bacall's) sister, saying, "You're not very tall, are you?" This gives Bogart a chance to quip, "Well, I try to be." While not precisely a film noir, *Anatomy*, thanks in part to these nuanced references and especially to the jazz soundtrack, carries the sense of noir into the rural settings, the courtroom antics, and even the end of the film, which takes place out at the trailer campground where the Manions live. Biegler and McCarthy head out to get a promissory note signed by Manion. As Biegler drives, McCarthy asserts that he likes the look of life without a whiskey sheen, and the men agree to go into business together. Ellington's "Anatomy" theme accompanies the big car as it pulls up to a lakefront site with an oil-barrel trash container filled to the brim in the foreground. The campground manager comes over and tells

FIGURE 7.9. *Irresistible impulses*

the two lawyers that the Manions left and that Mrs. Manion was crying. In a note for Biegler, Manion claims he is sorry, but he had to leave suddenly; "he was seized by an irresistible impulse." Looking through the top layer of trash, McCarthy disparages gin drinkers, while Biegler handles Laura's broken kitten-heeled shoe. He leaves it hanging on the edge of the trash bin. Pramaggiore describes the shoe as "the single, sleazy, sexy, broken shoe," that displaces "seediness, sex, violence and immorality all onto Laura," permitting the "male coupling" of Biegler and McCarthy at the film's conclusion.[54]

Biegler tells his new partner, McCarthy, their next job will be handling the estate of the murdered Barney Quill for his daughter. All the very gay places of northern Michigan no longer have to worry about Laura Manion. As the screen changes to gray, with the cut-up body from the opening titles, the jazz tune breaks off into eight high staccato trumpet notes, played by Cat Anderson, instead of a triumphant flourish or quiet fade to silence. Ambiguity abounds. The spectator never knows what psychic injuries McCarthy might have suffered or why Biegler never married. We never know whether Laura Manion was beaten and raped by Quill or beaten by her husband after she was with Quill. We know Biegler helped Manion discover his "irresistible impulse" defense, even though the evidence seemed just as powerful that Manion was a jealous and violent man who might have shot Quill for paying undue attention to his wife.

The film "received positive reviews and became one of the most popular movies of 1959 ... [with] *Variety's* year-end box-office wrap-up put[ting] it at number 7 for the year."[55] *Anatomy* also received seven Academy Award nominations, although none were for the music. Responses to the sound-track for *Anatomy* range from unimpressed, with the *Jazz Review* calling the music "uncommitted" and "lack[ing] in enthusiasm," to Stanley Crouch's glowing accolade, suggesting "the film score not only detailed extraordinary development but showed just how far Ellington and Strayhorn had stretched the language of jazz and just how far they were beyond all contenders."[56] Crouch sees it as a culmination that "brought forward much of what [Ellington] had been refining for over three decades."[57] Wynton Marsalis does not particularly like how the film uses the music but does suggest Ellington "was able to evoke feelings you've never heard in a movie. . . . One was the sound of sex."[58] Of course, for Hollywood, then and now, jazz always evoked sex. Marsalis goes on to say that Ellington's mature work on *Anatomy* is "among the most creative ever heard in jazz or film."[59] Miles Davis used the work on *Elevator* (*Ascenseur*) to stimulate his next musical exploration; Ellington and Strayhorn used *Anatomy* to play with the idea of themes and background music, using talented musicians to bring the score to fruition. Ellington used his band members as private inspiration. He and Strayhorn composed for individuals more than instruments, and Ellington tended to keep musicians for much of their careers. Nance worked with Ellington for twenty-three years, Hamilton for twenty-five years, Woode for five years, although he only worked with Johnson for just a few gigs, including the recording sessions for *Anatomy*. Jazz writer Nat Hentoff suggests that *Anatomy*'s soundtrack showed "above all, [Ellington's] commanding ability to use his orchestra as his own instrument."[60]

For me, Ellington's soundtrack suits the uncertainties of the narrative perfectly, infusing Ishpeming and its environs with an urban sophistication and cosmopolitanism that would otherwise elude the geography. The soundtrack serves the narrative by pointing to Hollywood's use of jazz in clichéd situations but at the same time pursues a separate agenda. As Domek notes, as "sound track music it's effective, and perhaps oversteps its role to the point of assuming a musical interest equal to the dramatic thrust of the film itself."[61] But I have been arguing here that jazz should overstep. In *Anatomy*, Ellington and Strayhorn remain true to their swinging compositional oeuvre and at the same time manage a detached but explicit commentary on the ambivalent morality offered by the film. As the closing credits run and the narrative comes to a close, the trumpet suggests, as David Grant Moss notes, a series of question marks instead of a closing period.[62] In classical Hollywood, the music and narrative insist on closure, but in late classic noir, the jazz soundtrack's alienation effect points to the tenuous nature of the requisite resolution and speaks about musical developments beyond the filmic narrative.

CHAPTER EIGHT

Cannoy's Club

"ALL MEN ARE EVIL"

*T*HE JAZZ CLUB SEQUENCE IN *ODDS AGAINST TOMORROW* (1959) opens with a medium close-up of Johnny (Harry Belafonte) singing and playing the vibraharp. That shot immediately follows the last words in the previous sequence, uttered by Earle (Robert Ryan), "You didn't say nothing about the third man being a nigger." This shocking transition points to the racism that will serve to undo a carefully planned heist.[1] The club—a haze-filled, sophisticated venue with racially diverse employees and clientele—features Johnny and a black band, including a bass player, pianist, and drummer. Jazz singer Mae Barnes plays Annie, singer and bartender at the club, and Cicely Tyson, in one of her early film appearances, tends bar and has a few lines of dialogue. No inkling of racism tinges the interactions at the club: the owner, Cannoy (Fred J. Scollay), and his body guard, both white, welcome Johnny into the office with authentic pleasure. The real threat to Johnny comes in the form of his gambling addiction and a gangster, Bacco (Will Kuluva), calling in Johnny's substantial gambling debts. The jazz club signals danger, not to the typical white protagonist of classic film noir but to a sympathetic black protagonist who is also a jazz musician and gambler. The diversity of the people at the club, the lack of any racism there, and the stylish and complex diegetic and nondiegetic jazz throughout the film represent Afro-modernism. Further, by breaking with Hollywood's stereotypical audial and representational modes, the film instigates an alienation effect.

Odds Against Tomorrow features stark and singular visual effects with glimpses into lives and locations peripheral to the central heist storyline. At the time of its release in 1959, Hollywood teetered on the cusp of color filmmaking, and *Odds* is director Robert Wise's last black-and-white film. John Lewis and the Modern Jazz Quartet (MJQ) provide an emotionally

FIGURE 8.1. *Cannoy's Club*

spare yet gripping musical score, both bleak and sophisticated. *Odds* deals directly with racial hatred; a Southern racist ex-convict teams up for a heist with a black musician overwhelmed by gambling debts. Like many noirs, it includes a New York nightclub scene featuring a jazz band, a crooked former cop, a well-dressed and cruel gangster with deviant henchmen, a loyal girlfriend, and a sleazy, sexy woman turned on by violence. The jazz band in the club represents jazz on screen; jazz musicians also lend their expertise to the soundtrack. Unlike most classic noirs, *Odds* provides a rare and tender glimpse into African American family life. Film noir often shows the family as threatened and helpless against the surrounding criminality and darkness, and *Odds Against Tomorrow*, as the title and the soundtrack indicate, makes the peril imminent and extends it to a black family. Although the derivative and didactic closing coda caused the reviewer in *Variety* to call the film "not altogether successful," it remains a remarkable example of late classic film noir and how Hollywood viewed and used jazz in 1959.[2]

Successful singer and activist Harry Belafonte, who Diahann Carroll called "the most beautiful man I ever set eyes on" and Eleanor Roosevelt felt "could mesmerize audiences in concert halls," produced and stars in the film.[3] For Donald Bogle, as an actor, he "lacked conviction and humor."[4] He seems convincing in this film, especially in the early sequences. *Odds* was based on a novel by William P. McGivern, who also penned another novel which became a film about threatened families and corrupt cops, *The Big Heat*; the concurrent reviews of *Odds* cite an African American novelist as the screenwriter. The reviewer for *Time* notes that the "tension builds well to the climax—thanks partly to . . . an able Negro scriptwriter named John O. Killens."[5] Killens had authored the activist novel *Youngblood* in 1954. In the remarkably valuable critical edition of the screenplay for *Odds* edited by John Schultheiss, director Wise comments that Killens, "a black novelist and friend of [producer] Belafonte's, was engaged to act as a front for [blacklisted] Abraham Polonsky."[6] Wise provides varying accounts of Killen's contribution, saying in an interview with Sergio Leemann that he "was the first person to do the screenplay," and yet later saying that he "never wrote anything at all of the screenplay; he just gave his name to HarBel to use as a front."[7] Nelson Gidding, the other credited writer, who had worked with director Wise previously on *I Want to Live!* (1958), wrote "minor stuff, not enough to justify getting his name on it" according to Wise.[8] In an interview, Wise recounts how he accepted the directing job for HarBel productions, Belafonte's company; Belafonte told him the writer "was a black novelist, and this was his first screenplay."[9] Then, when Belafonte brought "the writer over for [Wise] to meet . . . it was Abe Polonsky . . . who was blacklisted and couldn't get credit in his own name."[10]

An admitted communist, Abraham Polonsky was blacklisted in 1951 for refusing to name names during the House Un-American Activities Committee (HUAC) hearings. As Paul Buhle and David Wagner report, the leftist writer and director was identified by committee member and congressman Harold Veld as "a very dangerous citizen" for his refusal to testify.[11] Buhle and Wagner use the line as a title for their book about Polonsky, noting that the *Hollywood Reporter* used the line as a headline in 1951.[12] Before the blacklist, Polonsky worked on various noirs: he wrote the screenplay for a dark and gritty boxing drama starring John Garfield, *Body and Soul* (1947), and directed and wrote another Garfield vehicle, *Force of Evil* (1948). Polonsky worked anonymously from 1951 until 1968, when he received screenwriting credit for *Madigan*. In 1969, he wrote and directed *Tell Them Willie Boy Is Here*, starring Robert Redford. He did not get official acknowledgment for his work on *Odds* until 1996, when the Writers Guild of America awarded him credit, and according to the *Hollywood Reporter*, "asked the companies that own the films to change the credits on all future prints and videocassettes."[13]

Apparently, when the change in credits occurred, Polonsky called Gidding, and Gidding asked to have his name left on it. Since "Gidding had been graciously willing to act as a front . . . Polonsky decided to accept the wording of the screenplay" as shown in the 1996 credit sequence, which reads "Screenplay by Abraham Polonsky and Nelson Gidding" instead of "John O. Killen and Nelson Gidding."[14]

Wise, along with Belafonte, produced the film. As Wheeler Winston Dixon details, Wise had worked in Hollywood since the early 1930s, "editing *Citizen Kane* for Orson Welles in 1941" and editing and, notoriously, "later recutting and reshooting Welles's *The Magnificent Ambersons* (1942)."[15] Wise hired neophyte editor Dede Allen to cut the film, and the editing contributes substantially to the film. Allen would later edit countless award-winning films, including *Bonnie and Clyde* (1962), which was the first movie to have an on-screen credit for editing. She went on to edit many films for other directors, including films for Arthur Penn, George Roy Hill's *Slaughterhouse-Five* (1972), and Sidney Lumet's *Dog Day Afternoon* (1975).[16]

Wise had many films to his credit before *Odds Against Tomorrow*. For Radio-Keith-Orpheum (RKO) and producer Val Lewton, he directed the classic horror noir *The Curse of the Cat People* (1944), as well as *The Body Snatcher* (1945).[17] He went on to direct the "noir *Born to Kill* (1947) . . . the noir Western *Blood on the Moon* (1948), [and] science fiction classic *The Day the Earth Stood Still* (1951)."[18] Wise directed a series of other classic noirs, including *The Set-up* (1949), also starring Robert Ryan, *The House on Telegraph Hill* (1951), and *The Captive City* (1952). He would also direct *I Want to Live!* (1958) which features white jazzman Gerry Mulligan and black trumpeter Art Farmer—Ogden resident Betty Moore's cousin. Both musicians appeared on screen, in the credits, and on the soundtrack. Wise's experience with jazz in soundtracks began before *Odds*.

In *Jazz Noir*, David Butler uses *I Want to Live!* as a fascinating case study. He discusses the three categories of jazz in the film: Johnny "Mandel's jazz inflected non-diegetic score . . . the performances of the [Gerry] Mulligan and [Shelly] Manne band . . . [and] a number of miscellaneous recordings that are heard, diegetically."[19] Butler carefully researches and presents Wise's defense of jazz. Wise uses the Mulligan-Manne band, as well as the jazz-inflected Mandel score, to underscore the positive characteristics of the main character, convicted murderer Barbara Graham, played by Susan Hayward in an award-winning role. Wise champions modern jazz against the attacks of the film's producer, Walter Wanger, suggesting "she [Barbara] loved good music, from Brahms and Bach to Manne and Mulligan."[20] Wise's careful work with John Lewis, the composer for *Odds*

Against Tomorrow, makes perfect sense after reading Butler's exposition on Wise's support for jazz scoring in the earlier film.

Like the polished, professional Hamilton and the sophisticated, experienced Ellington, John Lewis provided Hollywood with a way to integrate jazz into the Hollywood system. As I note in chapter 6, Lewis scored *No Sun in Venice* (*Sait-on jamais* 1957), a French and Italian joint venture. Lewis realized his film-scoring task was innovative. In the liner notes of the album, produced using the music from the European film, Lewis talks about jazz in movies:

> Jazz is often thought to be limited in expression. It is used for "incidental music" or when a situation in a drama or film calls for jazz, but rarely in a more universal way apart from an explicit jazz context. Here it has to be able to run the whole gamut of emotions and carry the story from beginning to end.[21]

Christopher Coady provides a nuanced and detailed discussion of the music Lewis composed for both *No Sun in Venice* and *Odds*. He calls the former a French film noir, casting "its dark narrative strains against spectacular visual imagery," in this case the setting of Venice.[22] Coady then discusses how Lewis uses "composed music (a fugue no less) as a signal for deviance and vernacular-based improvisation as a signal of hope," shifting "the balance of positive associations in the film in favor of the vernacular."[23] Lewis does the same type of thing in *Odds*, with "Lewis sav[ing] the majority of improvised content to the second half of his film scores, capitalizing on a slow erosion of [film music] conventions in order to ultimately raise the overall level of vernacular presence."[24] Coady calls this Afromodernist. It also exhibits the alienation effect; jazz does not function here as it historically does in film noir.

Lewis's career has a familiar trajectory of early and long associations with other jazz musicans. Kenny Clarke, drummer on *Elevator to the Gallows*, and like Lewis a veteran of World War II, introduced the pianist and composer to Dizzy Gillespie after the war.[25] The musician joined Gillespie's "band as composer and arranger" and "received two degrees" from "the Manhattan School of Music."[26] With Clarke, vibraphonist Milt Jackson, and former veteran and fighter pilot Percy Heath on bass, Lewis started the MJQ in 1952.[27] No sources identify the men on screen in the jazz club quartet with Belafonte, but it is not the men who play on the soundtrack, Lewis, Heath, and Connie Kay. Unlike in *Anatomy of a Murder* or *Sweet Smell of Success*, I suspect studio bit players stand in for the musicians. In 1955, drummer Kay replaced Clarke and participated in the *Odds Against Tomorrow* soundtrack, staying with the quartet for the rest of his long career. Like Ellington, Lewis made his band a productive place and kept the same musicians together for four decades. Ellington wrote music specifically for the many remarkable players who worked with him— for example, composing not just for the alto or tenor saxophone but for Johnny Hodges or Paul Gonsalves. Similarly, Lewis insisted the MJQ "was a genuine cooperative, with each member assigned extra-musical duties."[28]

The MJQ reflected Lewis's "fascination with polyphony and counterpoint, and the conviction that J. S. Bach and blues were compatible."[29] Scott DeVeaux elaborates, noting that the "discrete, gentle swinging tonal structures of the Modern Jazz Quartet, performed by black men in tuxedos in concert halls for respectful audiences," suggested jazz could be "measured against the 'absolute' standards of greatness of the European tradition."[30] The European tradition also influenced Lewis's compositions, which were for a while identified as Third Stream by Gunther Schuller, "synthesizing elements in 'Western art music' [classical] with 'ethnic or vernacular [jazz and blues] music.'"[31] Schuller, a classical and jazz musician as well as a musical theorist, plays with Lewis on the *Odds* soundtrack. Despite the MJQ's "appearance and manner," both "genteel and cerebral," Gary Giddens and DeVeaux describe the music in *Odds* as "profoundly rhythmic and emotionally intense—in other words, cool on the surface, hot at the core."[32]

For Lewis, the score provided him with a new opportunity. As Royal Brown explains, he worked closely "with director Wise from the beginning of shooting, often changing his ideas as he saw the movie develop, but also contributing his own suggestions."[33] Brown elaborates, saying Lewis included the MJQ and "twenty other instrumentalists, including Bill Evans on piano and Gunther Schuller on French horn, to create a half-big band, half-classical score."[34] Jim Hall, who earlier played with the Chico Hamilton Quintet although he was replaced by Pisano on the *Sweet Smell of Success* soundtrack, contributes to the *Odds* music as well. Like Hamilton, Lewis managed to find work in Hollywood, producing or contributing musical scores to studio films. Both men were also concerned with liberating jazz from its cultural association with sex and sleaze, an association that classic Hollywood film noir had assiduously promoted.

Coady details how Lewis, in the earlier French film as well as in *Odds*, intentionally worked to both satisfy the generic sonic associations of jazz in a crime film or film noir and to ensure that those associations were undermined. As I note earlier, Coady sees this as part of the "AfroModernist paradigm, an ideology in which discursive strategies from outside the African-American cultural set are used during the act of advancing African-American presence."[35] Lewis, like Hamilton, desired to broaden the appeal and contexts of jazz. As Coady concludes, Lewis's scores for these films "were as much a result of his own compositional agenda as they were the result of developing compositional trends in the film industry."[36] While Coady argues specifically about Lewis's film soundtracks, what he suggests aligns well with my analysis of Davis's work on *Elevator* (*Ascenseur*) and Ellington's and Strayhorn's compositions for *Anatomy*. These men wanted and needed the economic boost that film work provided yet were also working on jazz, both as an art form and as a public offering to a larger audience.

After working with Lewis and the MJQ on *Odds*, Wise would go on to co-direct *West Side Story* (1959) with Jerome Robbins and direct *The Sound of Music* (1965), proving his facility with musicals and color cinematography. But it is his work in black-and-white that is of interest here. Wise's abilities with black-and-white cinematography emerge with the opening sequence of *Odds*, just after the main titles conclude. The wind blows across a puddle of trash-strewn water in a gutter. Soon a guitar joins the sound of the wind, and the camera cuts to an extreme long shot of a city street, with the gutter in the foreground. A cut introduces another long shot as a white man (Robert Ryan) walks into view. Despite the cool and windy weather, his face is sunlit, and the shot becomes a medium close-up from a slightly low angle. Another cut reveals a flock of birds flying overhead. Then back on the street, a horn joins the guitar as a mixed-race group of children, shouting and laughing, run with their coats flapping in the wind and their arms outstretched like birds. The man sweeps the last child, a little black girl, into his arms and lifts her up, saying, "You lil' pickaninny, you goin' to kill yourself flyin' like that, yes you are." Beautifully constructed cinematography is therefore contradicted by the dialogue's racism. The end of the film features the same music. As Butler points out: "Lewis' score ends with exactly the same musical phrase for Jim Hall's electric guitar; a sparse, stripped-down orchestration that gives the film a cyclical quality and suggests the same narrative pattern of hatred and mistrust will keep repeating."[37]

Volker Schlondorff reports this opening was especially valued by "French director Jean-Pierre Melville," and that *Odds Against Tomorrow* was one of several movies Melville showed regularly "in his own screening room to staff and friends."[38] The sequence goes on to further establish the man, Earle Slater (Ryan), as a racist and bully. Ryan had reservations about playing Slater. Ten years earlier, in *Crossfire*, a film I discuss in considering the liberal leanings of studio RKO in chapter 3, Ryan played a racist vet-

FIGURE 8.2. *Slater*

eran who, in an angry rage, kills a Jew. The film was directed by one of the "Hollywood Ten" who was blacklisted and jailed during the HUAC hearings, Edward Dmytryk. The novel that inspired *Crossfire* dealt with homosexuality, not anti-Semitism. Ryan was not anxious to portray another noxious character; in fact, the headline in *Ebony* shouts, "I didn't want to play a bigot." He changed his mind only after rereading the script and talking with his domestic help, the Smiths, about whether or not "Negros will identify [him] with the part of Slater."[39] He went on to note, "Most Jews harbored no resentment toward me for doing that part" in *Crossfire*.[40]

After the sequence on the street, Slater enters a hotel. Brown discusses the soundtrack, and this scene in particular. According to Brown, "Lewis' score provides a generally bleak, solidly dissonant, and sometimes overbearingly loud backdrop, without a leitmotif within earshot for this grim, black-and-white bank-heist drama."[41] Brown notes that instead of building "in texture and volume to what should be a whoppingly dissonant climax in the brass and timpani . . . the music stops right on a very obvious beat — Robert Ryan [Slater] slamming his fist on the hotel desk."[42] For Brown, the synthesis of the music and the action of the film is "usually a no-no, since it calls attention to the music."[43] Like Coady's suggestion of Afromodernist subversion, here Brown hints about what I call an alienation effect—the jazz does something other than what classical Hollywood scoring regularly does. Instead of building to a climax, the music stops altogether. Slater's angry demeanor and his underlying racism silence the jazz and clarify the politics of the on-screen action.

Meanwhile, Slater angrily badgers the hotel-keeper about not looking up immediately when he approaches the counter and then pointedly ignores a black elevator operator's friendly asides about the wind. Slater makes his way to a small apartment occupied by an older man, former police officer Dave Burke (Ed Begley), and his German shepherd, Uli. Burke welcomes Slater, offers him a whiskey, and, as the wind whistles outside the window of the little sixth-floor flat, complains that he "used to be able to afford a little space inside too." After a brief preamble that discloses Burke spent a year in jail on contempt charges and Slater served "two stretches, one for assault with a deadly weapon, one for manslaughter," the older man reveals a bank heist plan that will net fifty thousand dollars. He wants Slater's help. A phone call interrupts their negotiations, but it seems Slater will agree to do the job.

Johnny Ingram (Belafonte) pulls up to the same hotel, jokes with the same group of kids, and pays the same little girl Slater lifts up to guard his "little white Austin-Healy" before going into the hotel.[44] Slater walks

FIGURE 8.3. *Charming Johnny Ingram*

out as Ingram enters the hotel. In contrast to Slater, Ingram jokes jovially about the wind with the elevator operator, who whistles appreciatively at Ingram's fine sartorial style. Ingram makes his way to Burke's flat.

It is important to note the way the music plays a crucial but understated role in characterizing both Slater and Ingram early in the film. As Burke draws Slater into the heist, the timpani "builds tension against horns in a crescendo"; this motif continues out onto the street as Ingram parks.[45] Then vibraphone and flute "enter in an upbeat swing," associating Ingram with sophisticated, but lighter and more pleasing music.[46] For Coady the "vibraphone carries additional significance in that it is connected diegetically with Belafonte's character Johnny [Ingram] (a working jazz vibraphonist)."[47] Ingram at first refuses Burke's invitation to work the bank heist with him, saying, "It's not your line, Dave. That's the firing squad. That's for junkies and joy boys. We're people." But Ingram also acknowledges over seven thousand dollars in gambling debts, even as he politely refuses Burke's offer, and tells the older man, "You're in trouble. . . . Find a hobby, man, anything." So Ingram demurs, and Slater agrees.

Burke seems sympathetic, grandfatherly, and kind, but he makes sure that Ingram will sign on to the job. After Ingram refuses to help him, Burke goes directly to Bacco, the loan shark and gangster to whom Ingram owes money, and asks him to pressure the younger man. Bacco owes Burke some sort of debt himself, apparently for Burke's silence with the grand jury in the face of a jail sentence, and seems anxious to assist. In a brief sequence, Burke meets Bacco in a city park; the small man, neatly dressed in a dark hat and black overcoat, feeds birds as his two henchmen sit nearby on a bench, talking with a policeman about safety in the park. Burke suggests, "A fellow by the name of Ingram owes you," to which Bacco replies, affirming Ingram's charm, "Sure, a very entertaining boy at Cannoy's place." Then, suddenly the camera cuts from close-ups of the two men to a medium-long shot, and Burke takes a small but definitive leap toward Bacco. Their two dark figures loom against the white sky, as the birds suddenly flutter up and away. The cinematography subtly but emphatically emphasizes the threat they represent. Ingram will decide to work with Burke.

In the club sequence, Ingram plays the vibes, backed by a black drummer, bassist, and piano man. Black and white clientele enjoy the music as they smoke and drink. Bacco enters the club with his two associates. One of them, Coco (Richard Bright), lets Ingram know that Bacco wants to buy him a drink and then flirts openly with the singer, saying, "and I want to buy you a shiny new car." Gay characters are not unusual in classic film noir. Richard Dyer provides a list that includes Cairo (Peter Lorre) in

FIGURE 8.4. *Bacco and Burke*

The Maltese Falcon (1941), and Waldo (Clifton Webb) in *Laura* (1944), but Dyer notes that "iconography [marking gayness] is not explicitly sexual . . . [and] gays are thus defined by everything but the very thing that makes us different."[48] Coco exhibits the "fastidious dress" and "bitchy wit" used to signal homosexuality, but as this is 1959, he also overtly comes on to Ingram.[49]

In the earlier classic noirs Dyer discusses, the queer characters pay the price for their debatable masculinity, which usually links them to criminality. They, like the femmes fatales, will pay with their life or freedom, winding up dead or in jail. That is supposed to be mandatory, according to the Code. In fact, Shurlock reacts to the character of Coco, writing, "The character of Coco seems quite obviously to be a fairy."[50] Shurlock states that any "such impression would be unacceptable under the Code and could not be approved."[51] Even so, Coco remains in the script and film as a "fairy."

Despite his gayness and his criminality, Coco also apparently survives the narrative. The odds are against bank robbers; the gay hoodlum can go on his way. Shurlock could insist gays be eliminated from scripts and that no criminal or immoral acts go unpunished, but filmmakers, thanks in part to Preminger's interventions, now often disregarded the PCA's direction. In *Dames in the Driver's Seat*, I discuss gays in contemporary retro-noir films set in the classic noir period, such as *L.A. Confidential* (1997). I suggest that gay characters can survive the narrative precisely because they are men; while the female character must be punished, the male character might get away with transgressing without paying the price. It seems that *Odds* initiates that trend, although the women in the film remain so peripheral to the main plot that none of them seem to pay either. One character, Helen, for instance, gets away with cheating with her neighbor's lover without apparent guilt or penalty.

Ingram, however, will not be so lucky. The song he sings as Coco comes on to him is one of two original songs John Lewis wrote for the film, and it forecasts Ingram's succumbing to "the jungle outside my front door," as the lyrics suggest. The music underscores Ingram's descent into criminality and eventual destruction. At the beginning of the sequence, Ingram sings much like Belafonte might. Belafonte's popular success as a handsome crooner enabled him to start HarBel Productions. The film both capitalizes on Belafonte's public persona and undermines it. As the sequence develops and Ingram feels more cornered and threatened, his musical abilities lapse completely. He accompanies Annie (jazz singer Mae Barnes) in another Lewis original, *All Men Are Evil*, but provides only "off-key, out-of-synch, intentionally offensive intrusions" and then "flails and hammers at his instrument [the vibraphone] in a manner calculated to produce a singularly unpleasant sound."[52] For Holbrook, Ingram's character, up to now sympathetic, becomes much less so in this sequence.[53] Butler hears the music differently, suggesting Ingram's "music reverts to childhood and he bangs out simple chord progressions as if playing a child's toy piano"[54] In any case, the cacophony expresses the character's desperate state, and the singer Annie supports that understanding, saying, "That little boy's in big trouble."

In the club owner's office, Bacco threatens Ingram, insisting he pay his debt by the next day or he will "collect it from you· or that ex-wife of yours or your kid," and goes on to say that if Ingram does not make good, he will "kill you and everything you own." Ingram has an ex-wife and a sweet young daughter, but his gambling has destroyed his home life and now threatens those he loves. The threat makes Ingram desperate, and in a remarkable move for classic noir and classic Hollywood cinema of the time, the film proceeds to show the family Ingram will do almost anything to protect.

The sequence opens with Ingram's ex-wife, Ruth (Kim Hamilton), opening the door of her apartment. "You're late," she says, and then his daughter Eadie (Lois Thorne) runs up and "flings herself into his arms."[55]

FIGURE 8.5. *Ingram's family*

The little girl hurries out to call the elevator, and Ruth takes Ingram into the living room and introduces him to the "PTA steering committee," a group of men and women of mixed race and age. As Ingram stands at the door about to depart, the vibraphone starts, joined by strings. He leans in to kiss Ruth and does, but she turns her head to stop this show of tenderness. A sudden cut introduces a close-up of an almost frightening carousel horse's head and mouth. As the carousel wheels around, unsettling close-ups and shadows give way to Eadie and Ingram playfully exchanging kisses. But Bacco's thugs, hired to keep an eye on Ingram, wait on the periphery of the playground and interrupt the loving interlude. Despite the Central Park location, including the carousel and the skating rink, the unstable visual field and disruptive music infuse the whole sequence with anxiety. Ingram leaves Eadie eating at a counter and calls Burke to say he is in on the heist, horns "in a descending fanfare signal[ing] Ingram's acquiescence and descent into corruption and hopelessness."[56]

I cannot think of another film from the period that shows an African American family, however fractured, so tenderly and completely. Ruth's homey apartment, her concerns, her sweet young daughter, and the level of affection between a black father and daughter seem to me unique in Hollywood films of the time. In *The Big Heat* and other films noirs, white families might appear on screen. Providing Ingram with this nuclear family—a wife who cares for him but is concerned about his gambling addiction, a daughter who worships him—makes the black character well-rounded and sympathetic. Yet the film also shows his frustration with the white culture he sees Ruth attempting to accommodate, as he tells her, "Why don't you wise up, Ruth. It's their world, and we're just living in it." Ingram does not trust her "big white brothers" to make room for Ruth and their daughter. While Slater's misandry and Southern racism run deep, Ingram's fears likely stem from his life as a black man in America. Despite their reservations about each other, Ingram and Slater decide to join Burke. Neither man thinks he can live without the heist; neither can trust the other, and this leads to disaster for Burke's plan and death to all three.

Burke needs Ingram because he is black, but Slater does not know that initially or have any idea who the third man on the crew will be. The robbery depends on having a black man deliver food and coffee to a small-town bank after hours, as he does every week. The bank workers count payroll money on Thursday evening. Burke's plan involves gaining access to the bank via a side door, using the waiter—replaced by Ingram. Burke takes Slater up to the small town of Melton "about a hundred miles up the Hudson." The sequence begins as Slater takes leave of Lorry as a gentle piano and a flute play on the soundtrack, characterizing the lovers. Lorry tells Slater to take money from her purse and that he should not try to make it "just any way." Slater embraces Lorry and walks out to join Burke in his car. Now, the full complement of instruments (over twenty) join in a threatening crescendo, and the camera reveals various shots of the beltway from above. Wise notes that during production he was "fascinated with those ramps going over bridges" as he traveled from the studio in the Bronx "up the eastside to 125th Street."[57] Wise continues, "We got permission to go on top of one of those apartment houses right by East River Drive, saw this marvelous angle, and I shot clear across the Hudson."[58] Cinematographer Joseph Brun reports, "We used wide-angle exclusively throughout the picture" and adds, Wise "said to me: 'I want an atmosphere of increasing menace and a climax of catastrophe.'"[59]

As the two men drive, the music climaxes as a shot shows a road map with Melton underlined, and then continues in a disturbing vein. The realistic look of the town and surroundings has a documentary feel, but at first the dissonance of the music unsettles and alarms. The theme calms to a more consolatory mode, lending sound to a montage of shots of Melton: factories, churches, people going about their daily business, the bank, the bank clock, and the expanse of the Hudson in the waning afternoon. The montage concludes with a final shot of the bank clock, reading a few minutes after six o'clock. At first, the music imbues the car and criminal element travelling into the small town with dread. But the score for the montage of images of the town, while part of the same tune (labeled "Morning Trip to Melton" on the soundtrack recording), evokes a more uplifting and hopeful feeling. Brown notes that the music for *Odds* "is a consistently moody interplay of timbres and dissonant harmonies that strikingly parallel the coldness and loneliness of the film's winter settings . . . and the bitterness of its narrative."[60]

As darkness falls, the music that accompanied the montage ends. From an upstairs corner hotel room across the street, Burke and Slater watch a black waiter leave the drugstore soda fountain and walk down to the bank with a carton of coffee and sandwiches. Diegetic sound accompanies their observation, as they move from window to window, noisily abusing the metal venetian blinds to get a view of the action. Nondiegetic music, "timpani, snare drum and tambourine," accompany "Burke's explanation of the plan."[61] Burke closes with, "You could take it with a water pistol."

Later, during the actual heist, in a nice bit of symmetry, two youngsters with water pistols playing in front of the drugstore assist Burke in disrupting the waiter's journey to the bank. Meanwhile, in the hotel room, Slater responds to Burke's excitement about the plan with a line I quote earlier: "There's just one thing wrong with it. . . . You didn't say anything about the third man being a nigger." Censor Shurlock lets the filmmakers know that using "the word 'faggot'" and "the word 'pansy' . . . would be unacceptable," but the same is not true for the pejorative word describing blacks. Shurlock notes only that while "not necessarily a Code violation, we wish to advise you that we have been aware of a bad audience reaction to the use of the word 'nigger.'"[62] The word stays in the film.

As I note, from the hotel room sequence a cut takes us directly to a close-up of Ingram, singing in Cannoy's nightclub. Butler calls this "a trademark piece of Wise editing . . . [and] a textbook example of Eisensteinian collision," in that Slater's and Ingram's "lives are overlapping even though they have not actually met yet."[63] The cut underscores how Ingram and Slater, in their hatred and desperation, are more alike than they realize. And as Butler notes, Lewis's soundtrack explicitly connects them. Later in the film, Slater, checking out the power of the getaway car, "puts his foot down on the accelerator and breaks into a smile" accompanied by "an extended vibe solo played on the instrument diegetically associated with . . . the black jazz musician [Ingram] for whom he [Slater] has nothing but contempt."[64] For Butler, "what makes this sequence so striking is that Slater, a white racist, has his moment of emotional freedom accompanied by an improvised jazz solo. . . . Black jazz is used to convey the innermost feelings of a white character" and to link the white character in a sonically unambiguous way to his black counterpart.[65] The narrative and the sound-track reinforce the similarities between the men, rather than the obvious differences of race and demeanor. As we shall see, the conclusion of the film makes their similarities more apparent.

All three men meet up in Melton on the day of the heist. Slater and Ingram clash; Burke assures them the robbery will allow them all to "live again." They split up to wait until six o'clock. Wise notes that for this sequence, "As night falls [and] the three men in different spots wait . . . I used infrared film."[66] He adds, "It does distort . . . but gives that won-derful quality—black skies with white cloud—and changes the feeling and look of the scenes."[67] Visually, the sequence stuns the viewer with its seemingly documentary beauty. Ingram sits by the banks of the Hudson and watches detritus flow with the current. Meanwhile, in a park above the river, Burke loiters. He reads a monument plaque, sits on a bench, and looks down on Ingram below on the riverbank. Suddenly, Ingram sees something and gets up to look more closely—a dark-haired doll in a dress, its arm raised, floats in the water. The threat to his family contained in the action he is about to undertake becomes manifest. Here, the music re-sembles the earlier montage scoring, and once again gentle vibes chime in as the camera closes in on Ingram. Slater waits outside of town in the get-away car. He loads his shotgun, takes aim at a rabbit, and finally shoots it. The sequence ends with a picturesque sunset from Burke's elevated view, crepuscular clouds allowing the last of the sunlight through before the clock strikes six, ending the music and the visual interlude of waiting, and the lights come on in Melton. The music and visuals emphasize the beauty, mystery, and mundaneness of everyday life, for the people of Melton and for the men about to commit robbery.

As the film's title suggests, the heist does not go well. The plan hinges on one black waiter in sunglasses at night looking much like any other. That part works, despite the bank guard knowing the waiter by name. But Slater's violent personality and nervousness lead him to beat the bank guard and manager, and even the waiter, when he belatedly shows up. Slater also will not give Ingram the keys to the getaway car, breaking with Burke's plan. Burke has the keys but gets shot, and, unwilling to go to jail again, he turns his gun on himself. Shurlock, the censor, had attempted to intervene during the script phase, insisting that "Burke kills himself in an act of defiance against the law," in "an outright Code violation" that "could not be approved if it were to appear in the finished picture."[68] But Burke does commit suicide, much to Ingram's, and no doubt Shurlock's, consternation.

FIGURE 8.6. *Dead End*

Ingram blames Slater; they fight angrily and run from the bank. They wind up shooting at each other on top of oil refinery tanks, leading to an explosion much like the one caused by James Cagney's character in *White Heat* (1949) but also reminiscent of the nuclear explosion that concludes *Kiss Me Deadly*. The black waiter, Charlie (uncredited), had already mentioned the nuclear and automotive threat when he commented to some kids at the soda fountain before the robbery, "I don't know which is worse, the Atom Bomb or you kids and your do-it-yourself cars." As Slater and Ingram chase each other, timpani "and jazz cymbals counter in tense rhythm with snare drum sounding march roll[ing] underneath," until the cymbal "crescendo builds tension" to the climactic explosion.[69] For Wise, the ending of *The Defiant Ones* (1958)—starring Sidney Poitier—where racial hatred ends in mutual respect and even love, "seemed too pat, somehow."[70] He wanted to have the characters in *Odds* "both get lost in the holocaust at the end," showing that "hate destroys."[71]

And the similarities between the two men are reinforced once more. For the denouement, the ambulance attendant asks the police chief, "which is which?" as he looks at their charred remains. "Take your pick," the chief replies. Then the camera, in a shot that both evokes the opening puddle of water and the closing shot in *Citizen Kane*, pans down a chain link fence from a sign reading "Stop Dead End" to a black puddle of water, and we hear the sound of the wind and the same music that accompanied the opening sequence.

Although the Lewis soundtrack received accolades and resulted in two albums of music, it "did not result in a lengthy film career for the composer," although a few songs "would feature regularly in MJQ performances."[72] The same relative lack of Hollywood film employment played out for Hamilton and Katz, Ellington and Strayhorn, and Davis. For these artists, film work provided an opportunity to try out their compositions in a cinematic context, and the experiment proved rich if not productive of other opportunities in Hollywood.

Jazz itself disappeared from radio play or was relegated to late-night shows and struggled to remain popular and relevant with the advent of rock and roll. Nevertheless, due to Ellington and Strayhorn's sophisticated and detached score for *Anatomy*, Hamilton and Katz's stylish and urbane contribution to *Sweet Smell*, Davis's uncompromising pursuit of his own creative agenda in the service of *Elevator*, and Lewis's careful and thought-provoking music for *Odds*, jazz gains an association with intelligence and spectator engagement unmatched in previous films noirs or Hollywood film in general. Instead of only evoking emotions that support the visual and narrative flow of the film, jazz in the late 1950s films discussed here functions as a sort of alienation effect, underscored by the Afromodernist impulses of jazz at the time. Instead of asking spectators to only spectate, these soundtracks oblige the spectator to hear—to hear Davis's mournful trumpet and blazing bebop improvisations, to wonder about the eight brief bursts of trumpet sound at the end of *Anatomy*, to consider the meaning of the forlorn and lovely sounds that accompany the Melton montage. Butler calls this "a tantalizing glimpse of what might have been" had jazz been "allowed to speak for itself."[73] I do not disagree with Butler. In Hollywood, the cliché always overpowers innovation. Yet culturally, the progressive artistic contributions of major jazz artists to Hollywood productions helped change the way we understood jazz, racial prejudice, ourselves, and the future.

CHAPTER NINE

"Jeep's Blues" and Jazz Today

*I*N THE RECENT NOIR *AMERICAN HUSTLE* (2014), THE two main characters, Irving (Christian Bale) and Sydney (Amy Adams), connect through a shared knowledge of Ellington's death that year (1974) and a shared appreciation of "Jeep's Blues," recorded at the time of Ellington's career-reigning performance at the Newport Jazz Festival in 1956. The same performance likely made Ellington a good choice for Preminger to hire for *Anatomy of a Murder*. Today jazz remains a part of noir in Hollywood. *American Hustle* does not feature a complete soundtrack composed by a jazz musician, and the music used coordinates more with new standard Hollywood practice, e.g., in *Pulp Fiction* (1994), than the alienation effects of *Anatomy of a Murder* or *Odds Against Tomorrow*. However, jazz is there.

Sydney and Irving are classic film noir characters, grifters from the wrong side of the tracks, grabbing for more than they should. While the Production Code Administration (PCA) would insist that the characters in classic noir be punished for their excessive desires, neo-noir allows them to live and even thrive. In *Dames in the Driver's Seat*, I delineate a taxonomy of films that draw on noir themes. I identify retro-noirs, generally more reactionary in the treatment of race and gender, as films made today and set in the noir years, for example *L.A. Confidential* (1997). Neo-noirs, made and set roughly in the present, often offer revisions of gender roles, allowing the femme fatale to survive the narrative, as she does in *Jackie Brown* (1997). *American Hustle* uses the FBI Abscam operation as the basis for the story, set in the 1970s. I see the film as neo-noir. Despite Irving's elaborate comb-over and Sydney's fake English accent, I wanted the characters to survive the narrative, and they do. The film closes with Sydney and Irving again listening to "Jeep's Blues," having gone legitimate and

FIGURE 9.1. *Ellington as attractant*

managed to gain the family life Irving wanted. Jazz still figures in this noir, not as an indication or warning about the sleaze and danger of a certain milieu but to cue the spectator to appreciate and connect with the characters. A jazz tune is central to the narrative, but it only serves as part of the sonic landscape of the film.

This is to be expected. The heyday of true jazz soundtracks passed quickly; the alienation effect they engendered proved short-lived, like the jazz musician as Hollywood composer. After *Anatomy*, Ellington and Strayhorn composed for one more film, *Paris Blues* (1961), a film that featured Louis Armstrong and starred Paul Newman, Sidney Poitier, Joanne Woodward, and Diahann Carroll. Ellington's enthusiasm for the film, scripted to include an interracial romance, waned as he saw the revisions which avoided miscegenation. Ellington also worked on *Assault on a Queen* (1966) and *Change of Mind* (1969).[1] Strayhorn died in 1967. Ellington's musical career thrived after the 1950s despite the decline of swing, with his son taking over his band after his death in 1974. Davis composed for, played in, and appeared in various films after *Elevator*; he remained a creative jazz force until his death in 1991. Lewis composed for a few minor films, one in the 1970s and one in the 1990s, but the Modern Jazz Quartet worked actively into the 1970s and occasionally into the 1990s. Lewis stayed active in jazz until his death in 2001. Hamilton played and recorded jazz until 2013, dying the same year as Katz, his co-composer in the quintet and on screen in *Sweet Smell of Success*. Hamilton composed the soundtrack for *Repulsion* (1965) and, according to his obituary in the *New York Times*, also provided "music for television shows and commercials."[2] These composers and musical innovators thrived primarily without working for Hollywood, yet perhaps part of the shared cultural status of jazz as real American music in the most positive sense of the words comes from their brief and complex seizing of the screen at the end of the classic noir cycle in the late 1950s.

I have traced a trajectory in classic film noir jazz soundtracks from the sound of urban threats and sexual danger, or an intimation of white hipness, to a fully realized score working to fulfill the narrative necessities of a film and contribute to jazz music at the moment of its creation and improvisation. I suggest that jazz in late film noir asks the spectator to hear film somewhat differently. In his essay on dialogics and jazz, Gary Tomlinson seems to describe jazz in late classic film noir:

> It is the building of a precarious discourse that never fully displaces the other discourses around it. It is unsettling precisely because it defeats our natural impulse to be settled in the complacency of our own rules and terms. It threatens because it refutes the comforting idea of mastering a fully cleared space with open horizons in order instead to scrutinize the mysterious others crowding in on it.[3]

Hollywood wants us to be "settled in the complacency" of the movie theater, yet jazz insists that we "scrutinize the mysterious others" and try to make sense of what we hear. For me, that makes these films noirs from the late 1950s remarkable documents of our shared past and contributes to what I have called an alienation effect.

Nostalgia infuses the lyrics to Billy Strayhorn's "Lush Life" just as it infuses this project.[4] Ogden, Utah, where Joe McQueen played jazz with Charlie Parker and helped break the color barrier in nightclubs and where Betty Moore for a moment left behind the racism of her daily life as she watched Joan Crawford swept up in a kiss by a handsome leading man, serves as one of the "come what may places." No doubt there are others, all across the country. Real places, such as the Porters and Waiters Club in Ogden, and real jazz, such as that played by the musicians discussed here, informed the positive representations of jazz on film in the late 1950s.

The moment in *Out of the Past* when Jeff enters the Harlem jazz club evokes the Porters and Waiters Club. Later, Nat King Cole's sound makes it into Hollywood film, and even Cole himself, although his image is carefully managed and contained to eliminate the potential threat of a black man on screen. Yet he is there. For a moment, Chico Hamilton has the job of producing a soundtrack for *Sweet Smell of Success* before Hollywood gives the opportunity to Elmer Bernstein. Miles Davis takes a job composing for a film in Paris that would "ease the bite" of not having other prospects to play there, and he would use the opportunity to begin his modal explorations. Ellington and Strayhorn "live a lush life" while they compose for *Anatomy of a Murder*, and the soundtrack ties into the film, reflects the composers' musical concerns, and pushes the narrative's meaning in new directions. Lewis's contributions to *Odds Against Tomorrow* elevate that film to occasional sublimity. All these explorations in *Jazz and Cocktails* are fleeting instances in the history of race relations, jazz, and Hollywood. I express nostalgia for the energy, enthusiasm, and hopefulness of each of those moments and especially for those few films noirs featuring the sound of jazz scored by jazz musicians in the late 1950s. For me, those films still "burn inside my brain."

Notes

INTRODUCTION

1. Strayhorn, quoted in Hajdu, *Lush Life*, 34–35. Permission to use the lyrics granted by Alfred Music.

2. Hajdu, *Lush Life*, 34.

3. Kalinak, *Settling the Score*, 21.

4. Gorbman, *Unheard Melodies*, 2.

5. Fleeger, *Sounding American*, 138.

6. Strayhorn, quoted in Hajdu, *Lush Life*, 34. Some might dispute Utah's status as a gay place, but as chapter 2 suggests, that would be a mistake.

7. Unless otherwise noted, all film dialog is drawn from the movie.

8. Butler, "No Brotherly Love," 222.

9. Fleeger, *Sounding American*, 17.

CHAPTER 1: PIE EYE'S JUKE JOINT

1. Strayhorn, quoted in Hajdu, *Lush Life*, 34–35.

2. Fleeger, *Sounding American*, 17.

3. "Slim" escapes with Harry in *To Have and Have Not* (1944); Vivian Rutledge pairs up with Philip Marlowe in *The Big Sleep*; Nora settles in with Frank in *Key Largo* (1948), and Lauren Bacall marries Humphrey Bogart in 1945.

4. Cooke, "Anatomy of a Movie," 249.

5. Cripps, *Making Movies Black*, 44.

6. White, quoted in Cripps, *Making Movies Black*, 56.

7. Jones, quoted in Everett, *Returning the Gaze*, 304.

8. Bogle, *Toms, Coons, Mulattoes, Mammies & Bucks*, 121.

9. Portions of this chapter and chapters 3 and 4 appeared previously as "Jazz

and Cocktails: Reassessing the Black and White Mix in Film Noir" in *Literature/Film Quarterly*.

10. Everett, *Returning the Gaze*, 313.

11. Sobchack, "Loungetime," 155.

12. Wager, *Dames in the Driver's Seat*, 43–44, 48.

13. Wager, *Dangerous Dames*, 13–16.

14. Butler, *Jazz Noir*. Chinen Biesen, *Music in the Shadows*. Miklitsch, *Siren City*.

15. Lott, "Double V, Double-Time," 244.

16. Ward and Burns, *Jazz*, 334.

17. Kelley, "In a Mist: Thoughts on Ken Burns's Jazz," 6. Robin D. G. Kelley provides a cogent critique of the project of canonization and legitimization of certain musicians undertaken by Ken Burns's film.

18. DeVeaux, *The Birth of Bebop*, 25.

19. Knight, *"Jammin' the Blues,"* 15.

20. Lott, "Double V, Double-Time," 246

21. DeVeaux, *The Birth of Bebop*, 170.

22. Knight, *"Jammin' the Blues,"* 16, 26.

23. Gorbman, *Unheard Melodies*, 69

24. Ibid., 106.

25. Fleeger, *Sounding American*, 17.

26. Streeter and the other musicians "mimicked playing their instruments along with the pre-recorded track," written by film composer Dimitri Tiomkin and played by saxophonist Maxwell Davis, according to Dimitri Tiomkin: The Official Website (www.dimitritiomkin.com).

27. Kalinak, *Settling the Score*, 167.

28. Butler, *Jazz Noir*, 70.

29. Ibid., 70.

30. Ibid., 192.

31. Ibid., 193.

32. DeVeaux, *The Birth of Bebop*, 46.

33. Leonard, quoted in DeVeaux, *The Birth of Bebop*, 207.

34. Coady, "AfroModernist Subversion," 2.

35. Magee, "Kinds of Blue," 8.

36. Coady, "AfroModernist Subversion," 5.

37. Ellington, *Music Is My Mistress*, 47.

38. Brecht, "A Short Organum," 179–205. *Verfremdungseffekt* is sometimes translated as "a-effect," as "distancing effect," or as "estrangement effect."

39. Ibid., 193.

40. Ibid., 50, 193–194.

41. Ibid., 203.

42. Ibid., 203.

43. Mulvey, "Visual Pleasure," 40.

1. Brandon Griggs, "Jazzman Happy to Call Utah Home," *Salt Lake Tribune*, Apr. 25, 2005, http://archive.sltrib.com/.
2. "Utah: State and County Quick Facts," US Census Bureau, accessed Apr. 4, 2013, www.census.gov/.
3. Richard Roberts, "Ogden," in *Utah History Encyclopedia*, Utah Education Network, accessed Apr. 27, 2014, www.uen.org/utah_history_encyclopedia/.
4. Ibid.
5. Zoellner, "Dialogue," 13.
6. Davis and Tidwell, *Livin' the Blues*, 91.
7. Ibid., 92.
8. Zoellner, "Dialogue," 13.
9. Eileen Hallet Stone, "Living History: Does Utah Have a Rich Jazz History? Go See for Yourself," *Salt Lake Tribune*, Feb. 4, 2007, http://archive.sltrib.com/.
10. Kerouac, *On the Road*, 26.
11. Yorgason, "All Too Rare," 351–364.
12. Ibid., 353.
13. Ibid., 356.
14. Ibid., 357.
15. Ibid., 364.
16. Richard Seidel, liner notes, *Now's the Time: The Quartet of Charlie Parker*, Verve, 1989, compact disc.
17. Sedgwick, "Product Differentiation," 676.
18. Ibid., 695, 702.
19. Advertisement for Folgers Coffee, *Ogden Standard Examiner*, Nov. 6, 1941.
20. Reddick, quoted in Everett, *Returning the Gaze*, 289.
21. Weakley, quoted in Zoellner, "Dialogue," 13.

CHAPTER 3: STUDIO JAZZ FROM HARLEM TO ACAPULCO

1. Strayhorn, quoted in Hajdu, *Lush Life*, 34.
2. Gabbard, "Vanishing Love Song," 66.
3. Don Heckman, "Gerald Wilson Dies at 96; Multifaceted Jazz Musician," *LA Times*, Sept. 8, 2014, www.latimes.com/local/obituaries/.
4. Gabbard, "Vanishing Love Song," 66.
5. Ibid.
6. Guerrero, *Framing Blackness*, 28.
7. Cripps, *Slow Fade to Black*, 102, 354.
8. Ibid., 109.
9. Mapp, *Directory of Blacks in the Performing Arts*, 289.
10. "Caleb Peterson Plots Nationwide Negro Pickets," *Variety*, June 20, 1962, George P. Johnson Negro Film Collection mf, Margaret Herrick Library.

11. Gabbard, *Jammin' at the Margins*, 142–143.

12. Naremore, *More than Night*, 240.

13. Ibid.

14. In "Passive Masculinity and Active Femininities," a chapter on *Out of the Past* in *Dames in the Driver's Seat*, I discuss the complexity of the film's plot but focus mainly on Kathie's relentless activity, as she attempts to secure her fate, and Jeff's astounding passivity as he moves toward his demise. Wager, *Dames in the Driver's Seat*, 53–62.

15. Miklitsch, *Siren City*, 54.

16. Luhr, *Film Noir*, 102.

17. Black, *Hollywood Censored*, 299.

18. Shurlock, quoted in Doherty, *Hollywood's Censor*, 110.

19. Huston, quoted in Weinberger, "Joe Breen's Oscar," 386.

20. Leff and Simmons, *The Dame in the Kimono*, 296.

21. Ibid., 305.

22. Ibid., 287.

23. Ibid., 287.

24. Ibid., 287.

25. Ibid., 286.

26. Ibid., 299.

27. Powell, quoted in Koppes and Black, "Blacks, Loyalty, and Motion Picture Propaganda," 132.

28. Ibid., 133.

29. Ibid., 130–131.

30. Chinen Biesen, *Black Out*, 59.

31. Ibid.

32. Ibid., 70.

33. Koppes and Black, "Blacks, Loyalty, and Motion Picture Propaganda" 145.

34. Ibid.

35. Ibid.

36. Porfiro, "Daniel Mainwaring," 160.

37. Server, *Robert Mitchum*, 118.

38. Estimating script dated Apr. 3, 1946, *Build My Gallows High* files, RKO Radio Pictures, Arts Library Special Collections, UCLA.

39. Porfiro, "Daniel Mainwaring," 157.

40. Server, *Robert Mitchum*, 118.

41. Yannow, "Bop (R)evolution," 1398.

42. Script dated Oct. 4, 1946, *Build My Gallows High* files.

43. Ibid.

44. Ibid.

45. Daily talent requisition dated Dec. 11, 1946, *Build My Gallows High* files.

46. Lasky, *RKO*, 193, 195.

47. Ibid., 195.

48. Ibid., 202.

49. Production Code Administration files for *Build My Gallows High*, Margaret Herrick Library.

50. Ibid.

51. Ibid.

52. Ibid.

53. Black, *Hollywood Censored*, 308.

54. White, *Mitchum, Mexico and the Good Neighbours Era*, 23.

55. Script and letters refer to "Jose," not "José." Production Code Administration files for *Build My Gallows High*.

56. Luhr, *Film Noir*, 114.

57. White, *Mitchum, Mexico and the Good Neighbours Era*, 71.

CHAPTER 4: THE BLUE GARDENIA,
CLUB PIGALLE, AND DANIEL'S

1. Gunning, *The Films of Fritz Lang*, 390.

2. Ibid.

3. Bergstrom, "The Mystery of *The Blue Gardenia*," 98.

4. Gunning, *The Films of Fritz Lang*, 408.

5. Gabbard, *Jammin'*, 248.

6. Bosley Crowther, review of *The Blue Gardenia*, *New York Times*, Apr. 28, 1953, www.nytimes.com/.

7. Bergstrom, "The Mystery of *The Blue Gardenia*," 119.

8. American Film Institute Catalog, s.v. "The Blue Gardenia," accessed June 6, 2014, www.afi.com/.

9. Bergstrom, "The Mystery of *The Blue Gardenia*," 110.

10. Ibid.

11. Kaplan, "Women in Fritz Lang's *The Blue Gardenia*," 83.

12. In *Crime of Passion* (1957), newspaper woman Kathy (Barbara Stanwyck) publishes a similar letter and catches a femme fatale, dropping the woman with complete disinterest to pursue and marry the handsome detective (Sterling Hayden) on the case. Kathy will later murder her husband's boss (Raymond Burr, again!) for not promoting her husband. Kathy, like Casey, treats the criminal with disregard, seeking only the story.

13. Gabbard, *Jammin'*, 312.

14. William Ruhlmann, "Artist Biography," AllMusic, accessed July 1, 2015, www.allmusic.com/.

15. Gabbard, *Jammin'*, 245.

16. Ibid., 246.

17. Kaplan, "Women in Fritz Lang's *The Blue Gardenia*," 84.

18. Gabbard, *Jammin'*, 246.

19. Gabbard, "The Vanishing Love Song," 76.

20. Gabbard, *Jammin'*, 249.

21. Gabbard, "The Vanishing Love Song," 78.

22. Brecht, "A Short Organum," 71, 203.

23. Wager, *Dames in the Driver's Seat*, 63–71.

24. Meredith Drake Reitan, "'Another Giant Gone': Earl Grant and the Pigalle," *Lavenues Project* (blog), April 27, 2014, https://lavenuesproject.com/2014/04/27/another-giant-gone-earl-grant-and-the-pigalle/.

25. "People Are," *Jet*, Dec. 25, 1958, 42, https://books.google.com. "Entertainment," *Jet*, Oct. 7, 1954, 58, https://books.google.com.

26. Naremore, *More Than Night*, 241.

27. Ibid.

28. Life in Legacy, week of June 28, 2003, www.lifeinlegacy.com/2003/WIR 20030628.html#D43.

29. Hill, *Shades of California*, 235.

30. Ibid. According to Krin Gabbard, Ellington probably told dozens of women that he wrote that tune for them, as it was part of the seduction schemes that allowed him, according to legend, to sleep with two or three different women every week of his life. Gabbard, e-mail message to author, Dec. 2007. According to David Hajdu, Billy Strayhorn also deserves credit for the music, which Strayhorn meant as tribute to his mother, and "Satin Doll" was his nickname for her. Johnny Mercer wrote the lyrics. Hajdu, *Lush Life*, 141.

31. Silver and Ursini, *Robert Aldrich*, 351.

32. Williams, *Body and Soul*, 127.

33. Butler, *Jazz Noir*, 46.

34. Ibid.

35. Gabbard, *Jammin'*, 249.

36. Amott and Matthaei, *Race, Gender, and Work*, 174.

37. I elaborate on the concentrated use of jazz in 1950s noir in chapters 7 through 9, building a case for a more pronounced alienation effect produced by jazz club sequences and soundtracks in classic film noir.

38. Gabbard, e-mail to author, Dec. 2007.

39. Henley, the actor who plays Daniel, has an extensive filmography, having appeared in over twenty-five films, including *Ali* (2001) and *How Stella Got Her Groove Back* (1998), as well as numerous television programs, including NYPD Blue. Foxx also appeared in *Ali*, and more. He became a full-fledged celebrity, thanks to his Oscar-winning role as Ray Charles in *Ray* (2004).

40. Giddins and DeVeaux, *Jazz*, 411.

41. DeVeaux, "Constructing the Jazz Tradition," 501.

1. Butler, "'No Brotherly Love,'" 225.

2. Coady, "AfroModernist Subversion," 2.

3. Butler, "'No Brotherly Love,'" 225.

4. Naremore, *Sweet Smell of Success*, 33.

5. Ibid., 11.

6. Ibid., 12.

7. Ibid., 15.

8. Lehman would go on to write for Hitchcock in *North by Northwest* (1959) and contribute to the screenplay for *West Side Story* (1961) in a career that extended into the 1990s.

9. Naremore, *Sweet Smell of Success*, 31–32.

10. Ibid., 33.

11. Ibid., 33, 34.

12. Mackendrick, *On Film-making*, 123.

13. Ibid.

14. Naremore, *Sweet Smell of Success*, 15.

15. Ibid., 26.

16. Breen to Lord, May 16, 1949, Production Code Administration files for *Sweet Smell of Success*.

17. Shurlock to Hecht, Jan. 4, 1956, Production Code Administration files for *Sweet Smell of Success*.

18. David Denby, "Film Critic David Denby's Favorite NYC Movie Theaters and NYC Movies," *Latest Best of NY* (blog), CBS New York, http://newyork.cbs local.com/top-lists/film-critic-david-denbys-favorite-nyc-movie-theaters-and-nyc-movies/.

19. Naremore, *Sweet Smell of Success*, 46–47.

20. Feeney, *Nixon at the Movies*, 147–148.

21. Naremore, *Sweet Smell of Success*, 46.

22. Mackendrick, *On Film-making*, 3.

23. Ibid.

24. Rob Nixon, "*Sweet Smell of Success*," Turner Classic Movies, accessed Mar. 20, 2014, www.tcm.com/tcmdb/.

25. Naremore, *Sweet Smell of Success*, 46.

26. Gary Giddins, "The Fantastic Falco," booklet, 6–7, *Sweet Smell of Success*, directed by Alexander Mackendrick, originally released 1957 (New York: Criterion, 2011) DVD.

27. Ibid.

28. Sheri Chinen Biesen asserts the film was shot on location, including the 21 Club. Naremore and others say the interiors are sets, with the 21 Club as "the film's most expensive set . . . a perfect replica of the famous Manhattan eatery" where

Hunsecker rules over his domain like a major despot. Chinen Biesen, *Music in the Shadows*, 194. Naremore, *Sweet Smell of Success*, 61.

29. Yannow, *All Music Guide to Jazz*, 532.

30. Chico Hamilton, interview by Marc Myers, *Jazzwax* (blog), last modified Mar. 2, 2009, www.jazzwax.com/2009/03/interview-chico-hamilton-part-1.html.

31. Ibid.

32. Bill Milkowski, "Chico Hamilton: The Sweet Smell of Success," *Jazz Times*, Nov. 2002, http://jazztimes.com/.

33. Yannow, *All Music Guide to Jazz*, 1405.

34. Chico Hamilton Quintet and Elmer Bernstein, *Jazz and Orchestral Themes Recorded for the Soundtrack of the Motion Picture* Sweet Smell of Success, recorded 1957, Cherry Red Records, 2008, compact disc.

35. Feeney, perhaps because of his focus on Richard Nixon, makes a dubious connection between Nixon's and Sidney Falco's lack of scruples, misidentifies Katz as the piano player, and accuses the man of bearing "a somewhat alarming resemblance to Henry Kissinger." The inaccurate observation at least provides a chuckle. Feeney, *Nixon at the Movies*, 142.

36. Gabbard, *Jammin'*, 128. Meeker, *Jazz at the Movies*, 1905. Yannow, *Jazz on Film*, 203.

37. Chico Hamilton, interview by Marc Myers, *Jazzwax*. Hamilton humorously notes that "they alternately cut between John Pisano's hands on the fret board and Marty Milner's face when his hands were at his side. It worked pretty well, I think. One time I put my hands on the fret board and cracked everyone up. It stayed in too." The anecdote speaks to the atmosphere surrounding the jazz group on set. Hamilton, quoted in Arnold Jay Smith, "Octojazzarian Profile: Chico Hamilton," *Jazz.com* (blog), last modified March 3, 2008, www.jazz.com/.

38. Holbrook, *Music, Movies, Meanings, and Markets*, 267.

39. Ibid.

40. Milner would go on to varied television roles in shows including *Route 66*, *Adam-12*, and *MacGyver*.

41. Gabbard, *Jammin'*, 128.

42. Giddins, "The Fantastic Falco," 10.

43. Ibid.

44. Mann, *Hollywood Independents*, 224-225.

45. Odets and Lehman, excerpts from script for *Sweet Smell of Success*, 17.

46. Milkowski, "Chico Hamilton."

47. Odets and Lehman, *Sweet Smell of Success*, 17.

48. Ibid., 15.

49. Ibid., 20.

50. Gabbard, *Jammin'*, 128.

51. Ness, "A Lotta Night Music," 53.

52. Butler, *Jazz Noir*, 137.

53. Ibid.

54. Giddins, "The Fantastic Falco," 8.

55. Butler, *Jazz Noir*, 136.

56. Bernstein, quoted in Prendergast, *Film Music*, 119.

57. Butler, *Jazz Noir*, 137.

58. Naremore, *Sweet Smell of Success*, 48.

CHAPTER 6: A PARIS BAR WHERE MILES INNOVATES

1. Stayhorn, quoted in Hajdu, *Lush Life*, 35.

2. Coady, "AfroModernist Subversion," 2.

3. Malle, *Malle on Malle*, 18.

4. Frey, *Louis Malle*, 4–5.

5. Malle, *Malle on Malle*, 14.

6. Carrière, "Louis Malle, the Elusive One," 2.

7. Frey, *Louis Malle*, 3.

8. Ibid., 7.

9. Carrière, "Louis Malle, the Elusive One," 15.

10. Malle, *Malle on Malle*, 10.

11. Ibid., 11.

12. Ibid., 19.

13. Yannow, *All Music Guide to Jazz*, 309, 1405.

14. Malle, *Malle on Malle*, 19.

15. Davis with Troupe, *Autobiography*, 217.

16. Thanks to my friend Brian Whaley for that observation. Whaley, e-mail to author, June 2014.

17. Szwed, *So What*, 154.

18. Ibid., 151.

19. Giddins and DeVeaux, *Jazz*, 417.

20. Brown, *Overtones and Undertones*, 185.

21. Gary Giddins, "Extras," *Elevator to the Gallows*, directed by Louis Malle, originally released 1957 (Criterion Collection, 2006) DVD.

22. Malle, *Malle on Malle*, 19.

23. Malle, quoted in Szwed, *So What*, 155.

24. Cooke, *A History of Film Music*, 222.

25. Urtreger, quoted in Szwed, *So What*, 154.

26. Peter Watrous, "Recordings; Things Happened When Jazz Got on Screen," *New York Times*, April 23, 1989, www.nytimes.com/.

27. Ibid.

28. Ibid.

29. Russell Lack adds several titles to this list, including *Two Men in Manhattan* (*Deux hommes dans Manhattan* 1958), with music by *Breathless* (*À bout de souffle*) composer Marial Solal, and the earlier film *No Sun in Venice* (*Sait-on jamais, One*

Never Knows 1957), scored by John Lewis, pianist and composer of the Modern Jazz Quartet (MJQ). MJQ also included drummer Kenny Clarke. Lack, *Twenty Four Frames Under*, 203.

30. Holbrook, *Music, Movies, Meanings, and Markets*, 256.

31. Ibid., 255.

32. Ibid., 254.

33. Ibid., 254.

34. Frey, *Louis Malle*, 26.

35. Ibid., 28.

36. Russell Lack, in an otherwise fine discussion of jazz in the movies and Davis's work on *Elevator*, misidentifies the first murder victim as Julien's wife. Lack, *Twenty Four Frames Under*, 204.

37. Brown, *Overtones and Undertones*, 185.

38. Malle, *Malle on Malle*, 16.

39. Gorbman, *Unheard Melodies*, 27.

40. Brown, *Overtones and Undertones*, 186. Michael Freeman identifies the Davis record as a French release, *Miles Davis Group*, Barclay 10" LP 84018. Freeman to the Jazz Research listserv, Mar. 21 2013, "Re: *Elevator to the Gallows* and *Sweet Smell of Success*."

41. Carr, *Miles Davis*, 120.

42. Hayward, *Cinema Studies*, 102.

43. Malle, *Malle on Malle*, 16.

44. Roger Ebert, "*Elevator to the Gallows*: Malle's '*Elevator*' a Noir Masterpiece," Rogerebert.com, last modified Sept. 16, 2005, www.rogerebert.com/reviews/.

45. Ebert, "*Elevator to the Gallows*." Vincent Malle, booklet, *Elevator to the Gallows*, 21.

46. Malle, *Malle on Malle*, 12.

47. Ibid.

48. Kael, *5001 Nights at the Movies*, 215.

49. Phil Johnson, "Discs: Jazz—Miles Davis *Ascenseur Pour L'Echafaud* Fontana," *Independent on Sunday* [London, UK], Mar. 14, 2004, 28, Infotrac Newsstand (A114225068).

50. Gabbard, "White Faces, Black Noise," 263.

51. Ginibre, quoted in Carr, *Miles Davis*, 120.

52. Davis, quoted in Szwed, *So What*, 154.

53. Gabbard, "White Faces, Black Noise," 268.

54. Ginibre, quoted in Carr, *Miles Davis*, 120.

55. Carr, *Miles Davis*, 123.

56. Gabbard, "White Faces, Black Noise," 268.

57. Szwed, *So What*, 155–156.

58. Gabbard, "Miles Davis and the Soundtrack of Modernity," 156.

1. Strayhorn, quoted in Hajdu, *Lush Life*, 34.
2. Gary Giddins, "Extras," *Shadows*, directed by John Cassavetes, originally released 1959 (Criterion Collection, 2004) DVD.
3. Ibid.
4. Butler, *Jazz Noir*, 110.
5. Ibid., 116.
6. Townsend, "When Duke Records," 321.
7. Ellington, *Music Is My Mistress*, 193.
8. Hajdu, *Lush Life*, 188–189.
9. Fujiwara, *The World and Its Double*, 241.
10. Stewart, quoted in Hajdu, *Lush Life*, 188.
11. Ellington, *Music Is My Mistress*, 193–194.
12. Ibid., 194.
13. Griffith, *Anatomy of a Motion Picture*, 109.
14. Hajdu, *Lush Life*, 194.
15. Ibid., 57.
16. Ellington, quoted in Lawrence, *Duke Ellington and his World*, 349.
17. Domek, "The Late Duke," 80.
18. Ibid., 80.
19. Ibid., 84.
20. Ibid., 95.
21. Ibid., 117.
22. Ellington, quoted in Wein and Chinen, *Myself Among Others*, 157.
23. Butler, *Jazz Noir*, 130–131.
24. Ibid., 131.
25. Preminger to Shurlock, Dec. 8, 1958, Production Code Administration files for *Anatomy of a Murder*.
26. Shurlock to Preminger, Jan. 15, 1959, Production Code Administration files for *Anatomy of a Murder*.
27. Ibid.
28. Preminger to Shurlock, Apr. 29, 1959, Production Code Administration files for *Anatomy of a Murder*.
29. Shurlock to Preminger, Apr. 30, 1959; Production Code Administration files for *Anatomy of a Murder*.
30. Ballinger and Graydon, *The Rough Guide to Film Noir*, 199.
31. American Film Institute Catalog, s.v. "Anatomy of a Murder," accessed May 19, 2016, http://www.afi.com/.
32. Ibid.
33. Scholars identifying the film as noir include Raymond Durgnat, in "The Family Tree of the Film Noir," and Robert Porfirio, in an interview with director Otto Preminger in *Film Noir Reader 3: Interviews with Filmmakers of the Classic Noir Period*. While some call it noir, *Anatomy* does not make it into Alain Silver's *Film*

Noir: The Encyclopedia, although director Preminger does, thanks to *Laura* (1944), *Whirlpool* (1949), *Where the Sidewalk Ends* (1950), *The 13th Letter* (1951), and *Angel Face* (1953). The film earns fourth place on the list of the twenty-five best legal films according to the *American Bar Association Journal* in 2008. Nick Pinkerton, in the Criterion booklet, notes Preminger astutely released *Anatomy* "smack in the middle of the golden age of courtroom dramas that ran roughly from 1957 (*12 Angry Men* and Perry Mason's first case) to 1962 (*To Kill a Mockingbird*)," making it a courtroom drama with a swinging score. Durgnat, "The Family Tree of the Film Noir," 41. Porfirio, interview with Otto Preminger, 98. Silver et al., *Film Noir*. Brust, "The 25 Greatest Legal Movies." Nick Pinkerton, "Atomization of a Murder," booklet, 7, *Anatomy of a Murder*, directed by Otto Preminger, originally released 1959 (Criterion, 2012) DVD.

34. Fujiwara, *The World and Its Double*, 252.

35. Ibid., 248.

36. Leo Goldsmith, "Anatomy of a Murder: The Title Credits," *Not Coming to a Theater Near You* (blog), www.notcoming.com.

37. Keathley, "Otto Preminger and the Surface of Cinema," 2.

38. Ibid., 3.

39. Edward Kennedy Ellington, "Open-end Interview & Special Musical Platter with Duke Ellington," liner notes, 29–33, *Anatomy of a Murder Soundtrack*, Columbia, 1999, compact disc.

40. Pinkerton, "Atomization of a Murder," 12.

41. Keathley, "Otto Preminger and the Surface of Cinema," 4.

42. Sigmund Freud, *Civilization and Its Discontents*, 29.

43. Hajdu, *Lush Life*, 57.

44. Gabbard, e-mail to author, Sept. 23, 2014.

45. Gabbard, *Jammin'*, 192.

46. My use of Freud to interpret the behavior of the character may have been motivated by the framed picture of someone who looks like Freud smoking a pipe on the wall behind the couch.

47. Traver, *Anatomy of a Murder*, 248.

48. Internet Movie Database, s.v. "Joseph N. Welch," accessed May 19, 2016, www.imdb.com.

49. "'Have You No Sense of Decency': The Army-McCarthy Hearings," *History Matters*, American Social History Project, accessed May 19, 2016, http://historymatters.gmu.edu/d/6444/.

50. Griffith, *Anatomy of a Motion Picture*, 23.

51. Ibid., 52.

52. Maria Pramaggiore, e-mail to author, March 27, 2015.

53. Ibid.

54. Ibid.

55. Fujiwara, *The World and Its Double*, 245.

56. Crouch and *Jazz Review*, quoted in Tucker, *The Duke Ellington Reader*, 313, 442.

57. Ibid., 442.

58. Wynton Marsalis, "Music by Duke Ellington," liner notes, 12, *Anatomy of a Murder Soundtrack*, recorded 1959, Columbia, 1999, compact disc.

59. Ibid., 14.

60. Hentoff, quoted in Hajdu, *Lush Life*, 190.

61. Domek, "The Late Duke," 118.

62. David Grant Moss, e-mail to author, June 27 2014.

CHAPTER 8: CANNOY'S CLUB

1. The cut also points to the editing of Dede Allen, in one of her earliest editing jobs.

2. Unsigned review of *Odds Against Tomorrow*, *Variety*, Oct. 2, 1959, Margaret Herrick Library.

3. Carroll and Roosevelt, quoted in Bogle, *Toms, Coons, Mulattoes, Mammies & Bucks*, 190.

4. Bogle, *Toms, Coons, Mulattoes, Mammies & Bucks*, 190–191.

5. Unsigned review of *Odds Against Tomorrow*, *Time*, Oct. 26, 1959, http://content.time.com/time/magazine/.

6. Wise, quoted in Polonsky, *Odds Against Tomorrow*, 165. Dialogue is quoted from the film. Annotations to the screenplay and some critical commentary are from Schultheiss (137–298). Also included are commentaries on the music by Martin C. Myrick and Michelle Best.

7. Wise, quoted in Polonsky, *Odds Against Tomorrow*, 137, and quoted in Sergio Leemann, *Robert Wise on His Films*, 157.

8. Wise, quoted in Polonsky, *Odds Against Tomorrow*, 137.

9. Ibid.

10. Ibid.

11. Buhle and Wagner, *A Very Dangerous Citizen*, 145.

12. Ibid.

13. David Robb, "Blacklisted Writers Get Overdue Credits," *Hollywood Reporter*, Aug. 4, 1996, http://articles.baltimoresun.com/1996-08-04/news/1996217209_1_abraham-polonsky-blacklisted-writers-nelson-gidding.

14. Schultheiss, quoted in Polonsky, *Odds Against Tomorrow*, 317. Changes in credit sequence quoted from DVD versions of the film.

15. Dixon, "Robert Wise," 470.

16. Schultheiss, quoted in Polonsky, *Odds Against Tomorrow*, 148–149.

17. Dixon, "Robert Wise," 470.

18. Ibid.

19. Butler, *Jazz Noir*, 121.

20. Ibid., 119.

21. Lewis, quoted in Gary Kramer, liner notes, *The Modern Jazz Quartet Plays One Never Knows (No Sun in Venice)*, by John Lewis, recorded in 1957, Atlantic 1284, 2005, compact disc.

22. Coady, "AfroModernist Subversion," 12.

23. Ibid., 14.

24. Ibid., 15.

25. Megill and Demory, *Introduction to Jazz History*, 205.

26. Ibid., 205.

27. Ibid., 206.

28. Giddins and DeVeaux, *Jazz*, 348.

29. Ibid.

30. DeVeaux, "Constructing the Jazz Tradition," 500.

31. Schuller, quoted in Giddins and DeVeaux, *Jazz*, 352.

32. Giddins and DeVeaux, *Jazz*, 352.

33. Brown, *Overtones and Undertones*, 185.

34. Ibid.

35. Coady, "AfroModernist Subversion," 2.

36. Ibid., 19.

37. Butler, "'No Brotherly Love,'" 228.

38. Schultheiss, quoted in Polonsky, *Odds Against Tomorrow*, 138.

39. Robert Ryan, "I Didn't Want to Play a Bigot," *Ebony*, Nov. 1959, 68–70.

40. Ibid.

41. Brown, "How Not to Think Film Music," 3.

42. Ibid.

43. Ibid.

44. Polonsky, *Odds Against Tomorrow*, 24.

45. Myrick, quoted in Polonsky, *Odds Against Tomorrow*, 142.

46. Ibid., 142.

47. Coady, "AfroModernist Subversion," 16.

48. Dyer, "Homosexuality and Film Noir," 61.

49. Ibid., 60.

50. Shurlock to Stein, Feb. 23, 1959, Production Code Administration files for *Odds Against Tomorrow*.

51. Ibid.

52. Holbrook, *Music, Movies, Meanings, and Markets*, 259.

53. Ibid., 260. Holbrook plays the vibes, which may account for his reading of Ingram's playing as offensive.

54. Butler, "No Brotherly Love," 233.

55. Polonsky, *Odds Against Tomorrow*, 58.

56. Myrick, quoted in Polonsky, *Odds Against Tomorrow*, 149.

57. Wise, quoted in Polonsky, *Odds Against Tomorrow*, 145.

58. Ibid.

59. Brun, quoted in Polonsky, *Odds Against Tomorrow*, 146. In the production files for *Odds*, two hand-written documents attest to the filmmakers' devotion to the craft. First is a list of eight books on film aesthetics, including "'Film,' (Arnheim), 'Film Form & Film Sense' (Eisenstein), and 'Tech. of Film Music' (Manvill.)," as well as a list of eight books on film history, including "'A Million and

one Nights' (Ramsey) and 'The Film Till Now' (Rotha)" and "'Grierson on Documentary.'" The other document outlines the "5 differences between wide angle & telephoto lens." I suspect Wise suggested the books to educate John Flynn, his apprentice, and Flynn wrote up the lens cheat sheet. Regardless, the documents point to the filmmakers' understanding of film music, the documentary tradition, Soviet cinema, and their interest in all things cinematic.

60. Brown, *Overtones and Undertones*, 185.

61. Myrick, quoted in Polonsky, *Odds Against Tomorrow*, 147.

62. Shurlock to HarBel, Feb. 23, 1959, Production Code Administration files for *Odds Against Tomorrow*.

63. Butler, "No Brotherly Love," 230.

64. Ibid.

65. Ibid.

66. Wise, quoted in Leemann, *Robert Wise on His Films*, 157.

67. Ibid.

68. Shurlock to HarBel, Feb. 23, 1959, Production Code Administration files for *Odds Against Tomorrow*.

69. Myrick, quoted in Polonsky, *Odds Against Tomorrow*, 155.

70. Wise, quoted in Polonsky, *Odds Against Tomorrow*, 157.

71. Ibid.

72. Butler, "No Brotherly Love," 235.

73. Ibid.

CHAPTER 9: "JEEP'S BLUES" AND JAZZ TODAY

1. Ellington, *Music Is My Mistress*, 438.

2. Peter Keepnews, "Chico Hamilton, Drummer, Bandleader and Exponent of Cool Jazz, Dies at 92," *New York Times*, Nov. 26, 2013, www.nytimes.com/.

3. Tomlinson, "Cultural Dialogics and Jazz," 263.

4. Strayhorn, quoted in Hajdu, *Lush Life*, 34–35.

Bibliography

Articles originally printed in newspapers, magazines, or blogs appear in notes.

Amott, Teresa L., and Julie A. Matthaei. *Race, Gender, and Work: A Multicultural Economic History of Women in the United States*. Boston: South End Press, 1991.

Anatomy of a Murder. 1959. Directed by Otto Preminger. Criterion, 2012. DVD.

Ballinger, Alexander and Danny Graydon. *The Rough Guide to Film Noir*. London: Rough Guides, 2007.

Bergstrom, Janet. "The Mystery of *The Blue Gardenia*." In *Shades of Noir*, edited by Joan Copjec, 97–120. London: Verso, 1993.

Black, Gregory D. *Hollywood Censored: Morality Codes, Catholics, and the Movies*. Cambridge, UK: Cambridge University Press, 1994.

Blue Gardenia, The. 1953. Directed by Fritz Lang. Image Entertainment, 2000. DVD.

Bogle, Donald. *Toms, Coons, Mulattoes, Mammies & Bucks: An Interpretive History of Blacks in American Films*. 4th ed. New York: Continuum, 2002.

Brecht, Bertolt. "A Short Organum for the Theater." In *Brecht on Theater: The Development of an Aesthetic*, translated by John Willet, 170–205. New York: Hill and Wang, 1977.

Brown, Royal S. "How Not to Think Film Music." *Music and the Moving Image* 1, no. 1 (2008): 2–18. www.jstor.org/stable/10.5406/musimoviimag.1.1.0002.

Brust, Richard. "The 25 Greatest Legal Movies." *ABA Journal: Law News Now* 94, no. 8 (2008): 38–47. www.jstor.org/stable/27846942.

Buhle, Paul and Dave Wagner. *A Very Dangerous Citizen: Abraham Lincoln Polonsky and the Hollywood Left*. Berkeley: University of California Press, 2001.

Butler, David. *Jazz Noir: Listening to Music from* Phantom Lady *to* The Last Seduction. Westport: Praeger, 2002.

———. " 'No Brotherly Love': Hollywood Jazz, Racial Prejudice, and John Lewis' Score for *Odds Against Tomorrow*." In *Thriving on a Riff: Jazz and Blues Influences in African American Literature and Film*, edited by Graham Lock and David Murray, 221–239. Oxford, UK: Oxford University Press, 2009.

Carr, Ian. *Miles Davis: The Definitive Biography*. New York: Thunder's Mouth, 1998.

Carrière, Jean-Claude. "Louis Malle, the Elusive One," foreword to *The Films of Louis Malle: A Critical Analysis*, by Nathan Southern with Jacques Weissgerber, translated by Jacques Weissgerber, 1–2. Jefferson, NC: McFarland, 2006.

Chico Hamilton Quintet and Elmer Bernstein. *Jazz and Orchestral Themes Recorded for the Soundtrack of the Motion Picture Sweet Smell of Success*. Cherry Red Records, 2008, compact disc. Recorded in 1957.

Chinen Biesen, Sheri. *Black Out: World War II and the Origins of Film Noir*. Baltimore: Johns Hopkins University Press, 2005.

———. *Music in the Shadows: Noir Musical Films*. Baltimore: Johns Hopkins University Press, 2014.

Coady, Christopher. "AfroModernist Subversion of Film Noir Conventions in John Lewis' Scores to *Sait-on Jamais* (1957) and *Odds Against Tomorrow* (1959)." *Musicology Australia* 34, no. 1 (2012): 1–31. doi:10.1080/08145857.2012.681619.

Cooke, Mervyn. "Anatomy of a Movie: Duke Ellington and 1950s Film Scoring." In *Thriving on a Riff: Jazz and Blues Influences in African American Literature and Film*, edited by Graham Lock and David Murray, 240–259. Oxford, UK: Oxford University Press, 2009.

———. *A History of Film Music*. Cambridge, UK: Cambridge University Press, 2008.

Cripps, Thomas. *Making Movies Black: The Hollywood Message Movie from World War II to the Civil Rights Era*. New York: Oxford University Press, 1993.

———. *Slow Fade to Black: The Negro in American Film 1900–1942*. Oxford, UK: Oxford University Press, 1993.

Davis, Frank Marshall, and John Edgar Tidwell. *Livin' the Blues: Memoirs of a Black Journalist and Poet*. Madison: University of Wisconsin Press, 2003.

Davis, Miles, with Quincy Troupe. *The Autobiography: Miles Davis*. New York: Simon and Schuster, 1989.

DeVeaux, Scott. *The Birth of Bebop: A Social and Cultural History*. Berkeley: University of California Press, 1997.

———. "Constructing the Jazz Tradition." In *The Jazz Cadence of American Culture*, edited by Robert G. O'Meally, 483–512. New York: Columbia University Press, 1998.

Dixon, Wheeler Winston. "Robert Wise." In *Film Noir: The Directors*, edited by Alain Silver and James Ursini, 461–471. Milwaukee: Limelight, 2012.

D.O.A. 1950. Directed by Rudolph Mate. Cardinal Pictures, 2003. DVD.

Doherty, Thomas. *Hollywood's Censor: Joseph I. Breen and the Production Code Administration*. New York: Columbia University Press, 2007.

Domek, Richard. "The Late Duke: Ellington's and Strayhorn's Music for *Anatomy of a Murder* Considered." *Jazz Perspectives*. 6, nos. 1–2 (2012): 75–121. doi:10.1080/17494060.2012.721291.

Durgnat, Raymond. "The Family Tree of the Film Noir." In *Film Noir Reader*, 4th ed., edited by Alain Silver and James Ursini, 37–51. New York: Limelight, 1998.

Dyer, Richard. "Homosexuality and Film Noir." In *The Matter of Images: Essays on Representations*, 50–70. London: Routledge, 1993.

Elevator to the Gallows. 1957. Directed by Louis Malle. Criterion, 2006. DVD.

Ellington, Edward Kennedy. *Music Is My Mistress.* New York: Da Capo, 1973.

Everett, Anna. *Returning the Gaze: A Genealogy of Black Film Criticism, 1909–1949.* Durham, NC: Duke University Press, 2001.

Feeney, Mark. *Nixon at the Movies: A Book about Belief.* University of Chicago Press, 2004.

Fleeger, Jennifer. *Sounding American: Hollywood, Opera, and Jazz.* New York: Oxford University Press, 2014.

Freud, Sigmund. *Civilization and Its Discontents.* Translated by James Strachey. New York: Norton, 1989.

Frey, Hugo. *Louis Malle.* Manchester, UK: Manchester University Press, 2004.

Fujiwara, Chris. *The World and Its Double: The Life and World of Otto Preminger.* New York: Faber and Faber, 2008.

Gabbard, Krin. *Jammin' at the Margins: Jazz and the American Cinema.* University of Chicago Press, 1996.

———. "Miles Davis and the Soundtrack of Modernity." In *Cinema and Modernity,* edited by Murray Pomerance, 155–174. Piscataway, NJ: Rutgers University Press, 2006.

———. "The Vanishing Love Song in Film Noir." In *Kiss the Blood Off My Hands: On Classic Film Noir,* edited by Robert Miklitsch, 62–79. Urbana: University of Illinois Press, 2014.

———. "White Faces, Black Noise: Miles Davis and the Soundtrack." In *Beyond the Soundtrack: Representing Music in the Cinema,* edited Daniel Goldmark et al., 260–276. Berkeley: University of California Press, 2007.

Giddins, Gary, and Scott DeVeaux. *Jazz.* New York: Norton, 2009.

Gorbman, Claudia. *Unheard Melodies: Narrative Film Music.* London: British Film Institute, 1987.

Griffith, Richard. *Anatomy of a Motion Picture.* New York: St. Martin's Press, 1959.

Guerrero, Ed. *Framing Blackness: The African American Image in Film.* Philadelphia: Temple University Press, 1993.

Gunning, Tom. *The Films of Fritz Lang: Allegories of Vision and Modernity.* London: British Film Institute, 2000.

Hajdu, David. *Lush Life: A Biography of Bill Strayhorn.* New York: Farrar, Straus and Giroux, 1996.

Hayward, Susan. *Cinema Studies: The Key Concepts.* New York: Routledge, 2013.

Hill, Kimi Kondani, ed. *Shades of California: The Hidden Beauty of Ordinary Life.* Berkeley: Heyday Books, 2001.

Holbrook, Morris B. *Music, Movies, Meanings, and Markets: Cinemajazzamatazz.* New York: Routledge, 2011.

Ikenberry, G. John. "Creating America's World: The Sources of Postwar Liberal Internationalism." Unpublished manuscript. Last modified Sept. 19, 2005. May 7, 2014. Web.

Kael, Pauline. *5001 Nights at the Movies.* New York: Holt, 1982.

Kalinak, Kathryn. *Settling the Score: Music and the Classical Hollywood Film.* Madison: University of Wisconsin Press, 1992.

Kaplan, E. Ann. "The Place of Women in Fritz Lang's *The Blue Gardenia.*" In *Women in Film Noir*, 83–90. London: British Film Institute, 1994.

Kashner, Sam, and Jennifer MacNair. *The Bad and the Beautiful: Hollywood in the Fifties.* New York: Norton, 2002.

Keathley, Christian. "Otto Preminger and the Surface of Cinema." *World Picture* 2 (Autumn 2008). http://worldpicturejournal.com/WP_2/Keathley.html.

Kelley, Robin D. G. "In a Mist: Thoughts on Ken Burns's Jazz." *ISAM Newsletter* 30, no. 2 (2001): 8–10.

Kerouac, Jack. *On the Road.* London: Penguin, 1976. First published 1955 by Signet.

Kiss Me Deadly. 1955. Directed by Robert Aldrich. Criterion, 2001. DVD.

Knight, Arthur. "*Jammin' the Blues*, or the Sight of Jazz, 1944." In *Representing Jazz*, edited by Krin Gabbard, 11–53. Durham, NC: Duke University Press. 1995.

Koppes, Clayton R., and Gregory D. Black. "Blacks, Loyalty, and Motion Picture Propaganda in World War II." In *Controlling Hollywood: Censorship and Regulation in the Studio Era*, edited by Matthew Bernstein, 130–156. Piscataway, NJ: Rutgers University Press, 1999.

Lack, Russell. *Twenty Four Frames Under: A Buried History of Film Music.* London: Quartet Books, 1997.

Lasky, Betty. *RKO: The Biggest Little Major of Them All.* 2nd ed. Santa Monica: Roundtable, 1989.

Lawrence, A. H. *Duke Ellington and his World.* New York: Routledge, 2001.

Leemann, Sergio. *Robert Wise on His Films: From the Editing Room to the Director's Chair.* Los Angeles: Silman-James Press, 1995.

Leff, Leonard J., and Jerold L. Simmons. *The Dame in the Kimono: Hollywood, Censorship, and the Production Code.* 2nd ed. Lexington: University Press of Kentucky, 2001.

Lott, Eric. "Double V, Double-Time: Bebop's Politics of Style." In *Jazz Among the Discourses*, edited by Krin Gabbard, 243–255. Durham, NC: Duke University Press, 1995.

Luhr, William. *Film Noir.* Malden, MA: Wiley-Blackwell, 2012.

Mackendrick, Alexander. *On Film-making: An Introduction to the Craft of the Director.* London: Faber & Faber, 2005.

Magee, Jeffery. "Kinds of Blue: Miles Davis, Afro-Modernism, and the Blues." *Jazz Perspectives* 1, no. 1 (2007): 5–27. doi:10.1080/17494060601061006.

Malle, Louis. *Malle on Malle.* London: Faber & Faber, 1993.

Malle, Vincent. Booklet. *Elevator to the Gallows.* 1958. Criterion Collection, 2006. DVD.

Maltese Falcon, The. 1941. Directed by John Huston. Warner Bros., 2006. DVD.

Mann, Denise. *Hollywood Independents: The Postwar Talent Takeover.* Minneapolis: Minnesota University Press, 2008.

Mapp, Edward. *Directory of Blacks in the Performing Arts.* Metuchen, NJ: Scarecrow Press, 1978.

Meeker, David. *Jazz at the Movies: A Guide to Jazz Musicians 1917-1977*. London: Talisman, 1977.

Megill, Donald D., and Richard S. Demory. *Introduction to Jazz History*. 3rd ed. Englewood Cliffs, NJ: Prentice Hall, 1993.

Miklitsch, Robert. *Siren City: Sound and Source Music in Classic American Noir*. Piscataway, NJ: Rutgers University Press, 2011.

Mulvey, Laura. "Visual Pleasure and Narrative Cinema." In *Visual and Other Pleasures*, 14-26. Bloomington: Indiana University Press, 1989.

Naremore, James. *More than Night: Film Noir in Its Contexts*. Berkeley: University of California Press, 1998.

————. *Sweet Smell of Success*. London: BFI Film Classics, 2010.

Ness, Richard. "A Lotta Night Music: The Sound of Film Noir." *Cinema Journal* 47, no. 2 (2008): 52-73.

Odds Against Tomorrow. 1959. Directed by Robert Wise. Performance by Harry Belafonte. MGM, 2003. DVD.

Odets, Clifford, and Ernest Lehmann. *Sweet Smell of Success*. London: Faber & Faber, 1998.

Out of the Past. 1947. Directed by Jacques Tourneur. RKO Pictures/Turner Entertainment, 2004. DVD.

Phantom Lady. 1944. Directed by Robert Siodmak. Universal TMC, 2013. DVD.

Polonsky, Abraham. *Odds Against Tomorrow: The Critical Edition*. Edited by John Schultheiss. Northridge, CA: Center for Telecommunication Studies, 1999.

Porfirio, Robert. "Biographical Notes to 'Daniel Mainwaring Interview.'" In *Film Noir Reader 3: Interviews with Filmmakers of the Classic Noir Period*, edited by Robert Porfirio, Alain Silver, and James Ursini, 160. New York: Limelight, 2002.

————. "Interview with Otto Preminger." In *Film Noir Reader 3: Interviews with Filmmakers of the Classic Noir Period*, edited by Robert Porfirio, Alain Silver, and James Ursini, 87-100. New York: Limelight, 2002.

Prendergast, Roy M. *Film Music: A Neglected Art*. 2nd ed. New York: Norton, 1992.

Production Code Administration Files. *Anatomy of a Murder*. Margaret Herrick Library.

————. *Build My Gallows High (Out of the Past)*. Margaret Herrick Library.

————. *Odds Against Tomorrow*. Margaret Herrick Library.

————. *Sweet Smell of Success*. Margaret Herrick Library.

RKO Radio Pictures. *Build My Gallows High* Files. Arts Library Special Collections. University of California, Los Angeles.

Sedgwick, John. "Product Differentiation at the Movies: Hollywood, 1946 to 1965." *The Journal of Economic History* 62 (2002): 676-702. doi:10.1017/S0022050702001043.

Server, Lee. *Robert Mitchum: "Baby, I Don't Care."* New York: St. Martin's, 2001.

Sheridan, Chris. *Brilliant Corners: A Bio-Discography of Thelonious Monk*. Westport: Greenwood, 2001.

Silver, Alain, et al. *Film Noir: The Encyclopedia*. New York: Overlook, 2001.

Silver, Alain, and James Ursini. *What Ever Happened to Robert Aldrich?: His Life and Films*. Montclair, NJ: Limelight Editions, 1995.

Simmons, Jerold L. "Challenging the Production Code: *The Man with the Golden Arm*." *Journal of Popular Film and Television* 33, no. 1 (2005): 39–48. doi:10.3200 /JPFT.33.1.39-48.

Sobchack, Vivian. "Loungetime: Postwar Crises and the Chronotype of Film Noir." In *Refiguring Film Genres: Theory and History*, edited by Nick Brown, 129–170. Berkeley: University of California Press, 1998.

Sweet Smell of Success. 1957. Directed by Alexander Mackendrick. Criterion, 2011. DVD.

Szwed, John. *So What: The Life of Miles Davis*. New York: Simon and Schuster, 2002.

Tomlinson, Gary. "Cultural Dialogics and Jazz: A White Historian Signifies." *Black Music Research Journal* 11, no. 2 (1991): 229–264. doi:10.2307/1519944.

Townsend, Irving. "When Duke Records (1960)." In *The Duke Ellington Reader*, edited by Mark Tucker, 319–323. Oxford, UK: Oxford University Press, 1993.

Traver, Robert. *Anatomy of a Murder*. New York: St. Martin's, 1958.

Tucker, Mark, ed. *The Duke Ellington Reader*. Oxford, UK: Oxford University Press, 1993.

Wager, Jans B. *Dames in the Driver's Seat: Rereading Film Noir*. Austin: University of Texas Press, 2005.

———. *Dangerous Dames: Women and Representation in the Weimar Street Film and Film Noir*. Athens: Ohio University Press, 1999.

———. "Jazz and Cocktails: Reassessing the Black and White Mix in Film Noir." *Literature/Film Quarterly* 35, no. 3 (2007): 222–228.

Ward, Geoffrey C., and Ken Burns. *Jazz: A History of America's Music*. New York: A. A. Knopf, 2000.

Wein, George, and Nate Chinen. *Myself Among Others: My Life in Music*. Boston: Da Capo Press, 2004.

Weinberger, Stephen. "Joe Breen's Oscar." *Film History* 17 (2005): 380–391. www .jstor.org/stable/3815543.

White, Liam. *Mitchum, Mexico and the Good Neighbours Era*. Chaplin Books, 2014. E-book.

Williams, Tony. *Body and Soul: The Cinematic Vision of Robert Aldrich*. Oxford, UK: Scarecrow, 2004.

Yannow, Scott. *All Music Guide to Jazz: The Definitive Guide to Jazz Music*. 4th ed. San Francisco: Backbeat, 2002.

———. *Jazz on Film: The Complete Story of Musicians and Music Onscreen*. San Francisco: Backbeat, 2004.

Yorgason, Lawrence M. "All Too Rare: The Rise and Fall of Jazz DJs on Utah AM Radio, 1945-1964." *Utah Historical Quarterly* 77, no. 4 (2009): 351–364.

Zoellner, Mark. "Dialogue . . . with Anna Belle Mattson." *Northern Utah Junction* (May 1997): 13.

Index

ment of Colored People (NAACP),
11, 34, 36
neo-noirs, 4, 49, 58–60, 129
Ness, Richard, 70
Newport Jazz Festival, 96, 129
New Wave, 77, 79
Nichols, Barbara, 64
nightclubs, 11–16, 41, 49–50, 54, 60, 65,
112, 125, 131. *See also* jazz clubs
Nimier, Roger, 79–80
Nixon, Richard, 140n35
Nixon, Rob, 65
noir films. *See* films noirs
North, Alex, 11
North by Northwest (1959), 139n8
nostalgia, 1, 131–132
No Sun in Venice (*Sait-on jamais*, 1957),
82, 115, 141–142n29
nouvelle vague (New Wave), 77, 79

O'Brien, Edmond, 9
O'Connell, Arthur, 99
Odds Against Tomorrow (1959), 12, 41,
146–147n59; and alienation effect, 115,
129; casting, 112–113; cinematography,
117, 120, 124; and film noir, 4, 5, 111–
116, 120–123, 128; and jazz, 5, 111–116,
119, 125–128; and jazz clubs, 111–112,
115, 121–122, 125; origins, 113; plot,
118–128; score and soundtrack, 80,
82, 110, 112, 114–118, 124–126, 128, 132;
and sexuality, 112, 116, 118, 121–122
Odets, Clifford, 62–64
Office of War Information (OWI),
39–40, 44
"Ol' Man River," 34
opera, 2, 5, 17, 53
otherness, 9, 14–16, 18, 53, 58, 72
Out of the Past (1946), 8, 54, 62; and
alienation effect, 36, 58; "The First
Time I Saw You," 33, 45, 51; and jazz,
3, 31, 32, 33–36, 39, 41–43, 46–47; and
jazz clubs, 9, 33–36, 41–43, 45–46,

49, 77, 131; plot, 9, 33, 41–46, 69, 131,
136n14; script revisions, 41–47

Paramount antitrust case (1948), 11
Paris Blues (1961), 130
Parker, Charlie, 3, 21, 22, 27, 41, 67, 131
patriarchy, 13, 37, 63
Peery's Egyptian Theater (Ogden,
Utah), 29, *30*
Penn, Arthur, 114
Pete Kelly's Blues (1955), 68
Peterson, Caleb, 33, 34, 36
Petrovich, Iván, 84
phallic symbolism, 33, 36, 49, 59–60, 102
Phantom Lady (1944), 9, *10*
Pinkerton, Nick, 102, 143–144n33
Pisano, John, 68–69, 116, 140n37
Poitier, Sidney, 12, 130; in *The Defiant
Ones*, 127
Polonsky, Abraham, 41, 113–114
Porfirio, Robert, 143–144n33
Porters and Waiters Club (Ogden,
Utah), 21–32, 33, 55, 131
Postman Always Rings Twice, The (1946),
79
Poujouly, Georges, 84
Powell, Adam Clayton, 39
Powell, Bud, 27
Preminger, Otto, 4, 95–98, 100, 101, 106,
107, 121, 129
Production Code Administration (PCA),
2, 3, 11, 34, 37–38, 40–47, 60, 64,
97–98, 121–122, 129
Pull My Daisy (1959), 94
Pulp Fiction (1994), 129

radio, 11, 14, 18, 25, 27, 39, 55–56, 58, 128
Radio-Keith-Orpheum (RKO), 34, 41,
43–46, 114, 117
Railroad Porters and Waiters Club. *See*
Porters and Waiters Club (Ogden,
Utah)

matography, 65; critical success, 65; and film noir, 61, 63–65, 70, 74–75; "Goodbye Baby," 72; "Jam," 73; and jazz, 61–73, 63, 65–74, 96; and jazz clubs, 61, 63, 65–74, 77; location and sets, 65, 69, 72, 139–140n28; origins and screenplay, 63–64; score and soundtrack, 4, 61–62, 65–67, 69, 71–74, 94, 96, 115–116, 128, 130, 131; "Sidney's Theme," 67; "Susan: The Sage," 70, 72

swing, 11, 13–14, 21, 25, 31, 34, 130

Szwed, John, 80

Tell Them Willie Boy Is Here (1969), 113

Terry, Clark, 98

This Gun for Hire (1942), 14, 59

Thorne, Lois, 122

Till the Clouds Roll By (1947), 34

Tiomkin, Dimitri, 134n26

Tobey, Kenneth, 39

Toland, Gregg, 65

Tomlinson, Gary, 131

Touch of Evil (1958), 9, 90

Tourneur, Jacques, 33

Townsend, Irving, 95

transgeneric, 8–9

Trapeze (1956), 64

Traver, Robert (John Voelker), 95, 97, 99

trickster trope, 53

Turner, Lana, 101

Tyson, Cicely, 111

Un chien andalou (*The Andalusian Dog*, 1929), 53

Urtreger, René, 80, 81

Veld, Harold, 113

Verfremdungseffekt (alienation effect), 17, 134n38. *See also* alienation effects

Vincent, June, 14

Voelker, John (Robert Traver), 95, 97, 99

Wagner, David, 113

Wagner, Richard, 53

Wall, Jean, 83

Wanger, Walter, 114

Watrous, Peter, 81

Wayne, John, 105

Weakley Mattson, Anna Belle, 22, 24, 31

Weakley, William "Billy," 22, 24, 31

Webb, Clifton, 121

Webster, Ben, 2

Weegee (Arthur Fellig), 65

Weinberger, Stephen, 37

Welch, Joseph N., 106–107

Welles, Orson, 9, 64, 66, 114

West Side Story (1961), 98, 117, 139n8

White, Kitty, 56

White, Liam, 44, 46

White, Walter, 11, 34, 36

White Heat (1949), 127

Wild One, The (1953), 85

Wilen, Barney, 80, 82

Williams, Steve, 25

Williams, Tony, 56

Wilson, Gerald, 33–34, 35

Winchell, Walter, 63–64

Wise, Robert, 111, 113–117, 124–127, 146–147n59

Witness in Town, A (*Un témoin dans la ville*, 1959), 82

Woode, Jimmy, 93, 110

Woodward, Joanne, 130

World War I, 39

World War II, 8, 11, 13, 22, 29, 39–41, 90, 115

Wright, Chalky, 55

Yannow, Scott, 68, 80

Yorgason, Laurence M., 25–26

Zoellner, Mark, 22, 27